HERB MAGIC

HERB MAGIC

AN INTRODUCTION TO MAGICAL HERBALISM AND SPELLS

Patti Wigington

Illustrations by Mel Baxter

ROCKRIDGE
PRESS

For general information on our other products and services or to obtain technical support, please contact our Customer Care Department within the United States at (866) 744-2665, or outside the United States at (510) 253-0500.

Rockridge Press publishes its books in a variety of electronic and print formats. Some content that appears in print may not be available in electronic books, and vice versa.

TRADEMARKS: Rockridge Press and the Rockridge Press logo are trademarks or registered trademarks of Callisto Media Inc. and/or its affiliates, in the United States and other countries, and may not be used without written permission. All other trademarks are the property of their respective owners. Rockridge Press is not associated with any product or vendor mentioned in this book.

Interior & Cover Designer: Tricia Jang
Art Producer: Meg Baggott
Editor: Vanessa Ta
Production Editor: Matt Burnett
Illustrations © 2020 Mel Baxter
Author photograph: Aaron Werner/Werner Entertainment

ISBN: Print 978-1-64611-404-7 | eBook 978-1-64611-405-4

R0

FOR LILY BETH,

MY CO-PRIESTESS AND SOUL SISTER,
WHO ALWAYS JOINS ME IF
I STOP TO SNIFF PLANTS.

CONTENTS

➤ PART THREE: Spells and Rituals 85

ꝹNTRODUCTION

There's something powerful about inhaling the soft aroma of fresh herbs—it's an ethereal sensory experience that's reminiscent of an earlier time. Herb magic, also known as magical herbalism, is one of the oldest known forms of sympathetic magic, found in folklore all over the world. The herbs that practitioners historically used vary depending on location, as herbs were typically gathered locally. Someone living in one part of the world might have used completely different herbs than a person in a different region. Wherever magic was practiced, herbal knowledge was passed down for generations—first by word of mouth and later through written documentation.

Although we don't know for sure when people began using plants in a magical or spiritual context, author Scott Cunningham in his Llewellyn's Truth About Herb Magic *suggests that the Egyptians and Sumerians were using plants in magical ways by about 3000 BCE. We also know that the Greeks and Romans wrote extensive texts about using herbs and other natural items in religious rituals. By the 1400s, herbal magic and medicine were practiced side by side in Europe and other parts of the world.*

I encountered herbal magic early in my practice of witchcraft and spell-work. I had a friend experiencing medical issues, and I wanted to help—if I couldn't use magic to assist with healing, why bother learning about it? So I dove in and blended my first incense combination, using dried herbs associated with healing (a variant of this, the Healing Incense Blend, is in chapter 7). I lit the incense and sent my intentions out into the universe, letting the smoke carry them away. It wasn't long before I got a call from my friend, who told me that his symptoms had been alleviated and he was on the road to recovery. That was all I needed to hear. Since that time, I've used herb magic for nearly every purpose you can think of. As a practicing Pagan, witch, and priestess for over three decades, I've had plenty of time to play with plants. Whether it's to bring prosperity into my life, protect my home and family, or aid in divination, there's an herb out there for almost everything. I've been working with herbs for over half my lifetime, and it has been an empowering magical journey indeed.

We're going to explore 40 different herbs in this book, and then take a deep dive into what you can actually *do* with them, magically. Along the way, feel free to refer to the glossary at the back of the book if you come across a term that's unfamiliar. Remember, there are hundreds of different magical traditions, and each one has a slightly different set of beliefs and practices that inform the way herbs are used. The spells presented in this book are based upon the traditional folk magic practices of western Europe and the British Isles—and my own magical experience. Your own magical beliefs and experience may lead you to work these spells in a slightly different way, and that's okay! Do what you need to do in order to get the results you desire. It's my hope that by the time you reach the end of this book, you'll be ready to make your own herbal magic and join me in embracing a traditional practice that goes back thousands of years. I can't wait to share what I've learned over the years with you on the pages that follow.

PART ONE

MAGICAL HERBALISM

Magical herbalism has countless uses. Throughout history, people have worked spells and rituals to bring about healing and wellness—from curing warts and burns to saving the lives of new-born babies and their mothers. Herbal magic has been used to protect homes, farms, and castles, along with people and livestock, and can bring wealth and prosperity. Money charms have been found dating back to the classical period and beyond. We can use herbal magic for love—not only to draw it into our lives, but also to make ourselves feel more desirable. Herb magic can even be used to aid in divinatory practice, finding guidance and answers from other realms.

Anyone can practice herb magic with planning and a few simple supplies. In this section we'll cover the basics of what you'll need to get started, including the principles of herbal magic. We'll also discuss magical ethics, the various properties of magical herbs, and how to use them in spellwork. Are you ready to get started? Let's go make some magic!

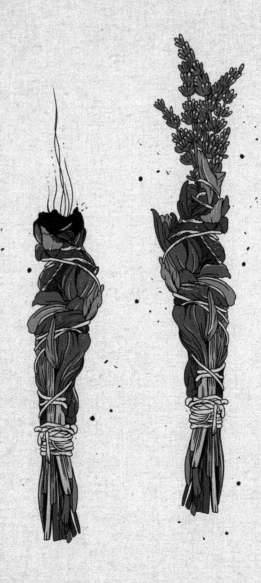

STRESS-RELIEF SMUDGE STICKS
page 121

CHAPTER
1

ⱣRINCIPLES OF ⱧERB ℳAGIC

Before really diving into herbal magic, there are a few important principles you should know. Many variables can affect the outcome when performing herbal magic. Timing, for instance, can be everything. The phase of the moon, the environment, and your location can influence magical workings. There are also magical ethics you might want to keep in mind.

The Basics

Magical herbalism has changed over the centuries. In the past, the only herbs a practitioner used were those they grew themselves or were able to gather nearby. Today the sky is the limit, because we have access to almost any herb we might need. If we can't find it locally, we can order it online.

Today's practitioners of witchcraft and other types of magic follow different paths and theories, and not everyone agrees on how or why magical herbalism works. Some people believe in a rationalist approach, which simply states that magic works because you *believe* that it does. In other words, the power of a flower, leaf, plant, or root is all in your head. Others believe the physical properties of each herb—the smell, appearance, taste, and so on—are where the magic lies, because they arouse our various senses to inspire magical thoughts. There's an animist theory as well: the principle that not only do all plants have unique energy vibrations, but they also have individual consciousnesses, and it's their spirit that makes the spell effective. In *The Green Witch*, author Arin Murphy-Hiscock points out that we can reach out and connect with the spirit of a plant, and then ask the plant itself for information about its properties and use.

Although my practice is rooted in traditional American and European folk magic, yours might be from another part of the world. You'll find, however, that magical correspondences are often universal across cultures. This book is based upon these common magical correspondences and energy properties; they are the basis of sympathetic magic and found the world over. Keep in mind that in this book we'll be focusing on folkloric and magical uses of herbs, rather than on medicinal applications.

A correspondence is the way in which an object represents another object, person, or concept. It's why we associate rosemary with remembrance and mugwort with divination or psychic abilities. The idea of magical correspondences can be traced back to the doctrine of signatures and the time of the Greek physician Dioscorides, who lived in the first century CE. Dioscorides, a pharmacologist and botanist, proposed that certain plants could be used to treat illnesses in body parts to which they held a resemblance. For example, walnuts might be used to treat ailments of the human brain—after all, if you crack open a walnut shell and look at the nut inside, it looks a lot like what's in our skulls. During the seventeenth century, European physicians and philosophers took the idea a step further and ascribed theological meanings to these correspondences; they believed that if God had created plants with specific correspondences, then God must have wanted humans to treat the related disease. By selecting plants that are the right fit for your purposes, you're stacking the magical odds in your favor.

This book is meant to be a guide to getting started with herbal spellwork. Although there are many types of baneful, or negative, magic that can be done with herbs, we're not going to cover them in this book. Instead, we're going to focus on more positive purposes—spells for magical intentions like healing, love, prosperity, and protection. We'll discuss magic for divination, intuition, and developing your psychic gifts. Rest assured, if you're interested in delving deeper into the world of magical herbalism, there are numerous books available to help grow your knowledge. Review the Resources and References sections for reading recommendations.

Magical Ethics

Each of us has different ethical guidelines. These are the principles we stand by no matter what. In magic, there is a general set of ethical guidelines that most practitioners follow. Although you'll find these ethical tenets vary from one magical tradition to another, there are several common threads:

♦ Don't deliberately cause harm to other people or use magic to take advantage of others; don't do baneful magic without good reason.

♦ Accept responsibility for your words and actions. Admit your mistakes and learn from them.

♦ You almost always get back what you give out. Put out positivity, and you'll reap the benefits. Do nothing but negative, and that's what you'll see in return.

♦ Magic requires effort. If you're not willing to study, do the work, and learn from your practice, then you're not ready for magic.

♦ If you're opposed to a particular type of spell, and it violates your personal code of standards, don't do it.

Timing

When it comes to magic, many practitioners feel timing is important. While there's no hard and fast rule that you *have* to follow timing guidelines, you may find your spellwork more effective if you do. Write down when you're doing a working—include the date, the time, the day of the week, and the moon phase.

Each weekday has its own unique set of associations. For instance, Sunday is tied to hope, beauty, and creativity, while Monday relates to purity, healing, and intuitive gifts. If you need to work on protection, conflict, or marriage, Tuesday is the day for those, but Wednesday is a good time for spells connected to communication and travel. On Thursday, focus your efforts on family, success, and prosperity, and reserve Friday for magic associated with fertility, harmony, and personal growth. Wrap up your week on Saturday with good fortune spells and the banishment of negative energy.

Moon phases can make a difference as well. The waxing moon—the period when the moon goes from dark to full—is a great time to do magic that attracts things. On the other hand, the waning moon is associated with banishing. For instance, if you wanted to attract money, do a working during the waxing moon—but to eliminate debt, cast a spell in the waning phase. The full moon is a period of extra power, and can be used for magic involving divination, psychic development, and inner wisdom.

Ultimately, the best time to do a magical working of any sort is when you need it. For more details on timing, be sure to consult some of the herb magic books in the Resources and References sections.

YOUR MAGICAL ALTAR

People in many magical belief systems use an altar as the foundation of their practice. Your magical altar is a uniquely personal place and can include all sorts of things that you find useful, but it is essentially the focus of religious ceremony and the center of spellcasting. Your altar might contain some of the following items:

◆ Magical tools for your belief system—do you use a wand, a knife, or a cauldron?

◆ Candles are sometimes used to represent the gods and goddesses of a given belief system, or you can use candles to symbolize the four directions: north, south, east, and west.

♦ If you write down your spells and rituals, keep your Book of Shadows, the personal spell book found in many Pagan traditions, on your altar.

♦ Items to represent the four classical elements: a dish of soil or sand for earth, incense or a feather for air, a candle to symbolize fire, and a chalice or goblet of consecrated water.

Environment

In addition to *when* you do your magical workings, *where* you do them can be important. Many practitioners do their magical work at an altar, but whatever you call your workspace, it needs to be somewhere you can work undisturbed. If you're in the middle of a spell and the phone is ringing, the dog is barking, and your kids are fighting over the remote, your working is going to be less than effective—if it works at all. Instead, make sure your workspace is in a private area of your home—your bedroom, the living room, or wherever works best for you. Some people find, especially with herbal magic, that outdoors works best for them; if you have the luxury of a peaceful spot in your yard where you can make magic, go for it!

In many magical traditions, the altar or magical workspace is positioned to face a specific direction. Many people like to orient their workspace to face east, because this is the direction of the rising sun. In some modern belief systems, altars face to the north, because that's where ritual begins.

You can also adjust your location based upon the type of spell you're casting. Those related to stability and security can be performed facing north, associated with the element of earth, while spellwork related to communication and wisdom might be done facing east, because it's connected to the element of air. If you face the south, associated with fire, you might want to do workings related to power, strong will, and energy. Finally, if you're doing spellwork for healing, cleansing, or purification, face west, where the element of water resides.

Planning and Preparing

Depending on your magical tradition or belief system, you may want to get into the habit of doing some of the actions discussed in this section prior to performing herb magic. The key is to figure out what works best for you and stick with it.

People in some traditions like to take a ritual cleansing bath prior to performing magic. Simply run a warm bath and place a cloth bag filled with purification and cleansing herbs under the faucet. Consider adding white candles and meditating quietly while you're in the tub.

You might want to wear ceremonial clothing for your herb magic. For many practitioners, including those following a Druid tradition, this is a ritual robe, but wear anything you're comfortable with. A ritual robe is often white but can be any color that resonates with you. It is typically made of muslin or cotton, plain and unadorned by decoration or fancy trimmings. Most people find it helps to wear something special, not everyday clothing.

Avoid wearing watches or other electronic devices, and leave your cell phone out of your workspace. Some people opt to abstain from sex, alcohol, and even food prior to working magic. Do this if you wish, or if you find it works better for you, but there's no universal rule about abstinence.

Finally, you may find some value in creating sacred space by casting a circle around your work area. Casting a circle is a traditional way of delineating your workspace as sacred before you get started with spellwork or ritual. There are a number of ways to do this, but if you're working with herbs, you can incorporate them into the process. One of the simplest ways is to walk around your workspace in a clockwise direction, pausing at each of the four points on a compass, and asking the spirits of the associated elements—earth for north, air for east, fire for south, and water for west—to watch over your space and keep it safe.

Visualization

For many practitioners, visualization is a key component of their spellwork. The principle behind visualization is a simple one: If you focus your mind on your end goal, it becomes achievable. Positive visualization, which relies on basic meditative techniques, is a great way to guide your herbal magic to a successful result. You may already have a method of visualization you're using successfully; use what works best for you.

How you use visualization is up to you. Some people prefer outcome-based visualization, in which you imagine the final result. For instance, if you're doing a protection spell, like the Peaceful Protection Potted Plant (page 96), you might visualize the outcome of a safe, secure, and well-guarded home.

Others use visualization that is more process-oriented, focusing on each step in the journey rather than the ultimate destination. If this is a method you like, you can work on the Peaceful Protection Potted Plant spell by visualizing yourself placing the hematite stones in the pot, adding the warm fresh soil, placing the rosemary seedling into the soil, and so forth.

When you visualize events and results in great detail, your brain begins to believe they're actually happening—it doesn't always know the difference between reality and your imagination. By creating this experience in your mind, you'll make the magic more effective; this follows the old adage, *If you believe it, you can achieve it.* In other words, focus and energy lead to a more successful result.

DIVINATION DREAM SACHET
page 148

CHAPTER
2

ABOUT MAGIC HERBS

Herbs are living, breathing things, each with a unique energy vibration, or signature. Knowing their magical properties will help you choose which herbs to use for specific magical purposes.

Bear in mind that this book is an introductory one, so we won't be diving into the deeper complexities of things like planetary and elemental rulers, or herb gender. However, it's important to have a rudimentary knowledge of how these properties, as well as things like color and magical intent, will impact the end result of your workings.

The Power of Herbs

How did we start using herbs in so many ways? Human beings have always used plants as more than just fancy flavoring for their foods. Roots, leaves, flowers, and stems have been incorporated into medicine as far back as the Paleolithic Period. In more recent times—some four to five thousand years ago—the Sumerians and Egyptians wrote detailed medical texts involving the use of herbs. The ancient Greeks, Romans, and Chinese all used herbal medicine. Over the centuries, people began to notice that various plants treated different illnesses, and they passed that knowledge down from generation to generation. During the Middle Ages, Arabic travelers shared information with European physicians, and the use of herbs as medicine evolved into a science.

From a magical perspective, there is plenty of potential in just about everything you stock in your kitchen. Once you start practicing herbal magic, the possibilities are endless; there's not much you can't do with a well-stocked herbal pantry. Imagine, for just a moment, making changes in all of the parts of your life you find dissatisfying. What if you could bring love into your world, heal a sick friend, protect your home from danger, and invite financial abundance your way, just by working with plants?

You can. That's what magical herbalism is all about. It allows us to harness the magical powers of plants—from root to flower to seed—to empower and enrich our own lives.

Magic Herbs

So what makes an herb magical? In some cases, plants are seen as magical because of their healing properties. These healing herbs have gained their magical reputation because they work to cure ailments. Common milkweed, or *asclepias syriaca,* which oozes a sticky white sap and was used by early medical practitioners to stimulate milk production in new mothers, is used in magic to protect women and babies after childbirth. Feverfew, an herb historically used in tea to bring down a fever, is associated with healing magic thanks to its medical usage throughout the ages.

Herbs are magical for other reasons, too. In ethnobotanical studies of plants sacred to various indigenous groups, some herbs are afforded the status of "magical" for historical and cultural reasons. For instance, Herbert C. Covey says in *African American Slave Medicine* that cotton root bark, used in some parts of Africa to treat a variety of female complaints, traveled across the Atlantic with enslaved women, and in North America it was used to prevent conception after assault by white slave owners. Covey goes on to say that cotton root bark has become a sacred herb to people in many African traditional practices because of the way it protected practitioners' ancestors.

According to Oxford professor Ronald Hutton in *The Triumph of the Moon,* mistletoe became associated with magical uses thanks to the Druids, who used it in sacred rituals, particularly around the winter solstice. Pliny the Elder wrote in his *Natural History* that mistletoe was a rare and sacred plant, gathered with much ceremony by Druid priests before ritual sacrifice.

ENDANGERED HERBS

Today, many practitioners of magic purchase herbs commercially. In some cases, increasing demand has led to plants like ginseng, white sage, and Palo Santo becoming endangered. In cases where you need to do a working with an endangered or at-risk herb, consider whether there might be acceptable substitutions. Look for alternatives containing the same magical properties. You can also help maintain supplies by growing your own herbs. Even if you have only a small container garden in your windowsill, it's a good start. In addition, growing your own herbs helps you become more connected to them. Finally, be a responsible consumer—learn which herbs are endangered or unethically sourced and find ways to avoid using them altogether. Do research online or check with a local agricultural extension to see what herbs shouldn't be gathered in your area.

TOXIC AND DANGEROUS HERBS

Some herbs are unsafe to handle or ingest because they are dangerous for both humans and animals. If you're pregnant, attempting to become pregnant, or nursing, be extra careful when working with herbs. Plants like comfrey, pennyroyal, and mistletoe can cause miscarriage. If you've got pets, don't leave herbs in places they can reach. Cats in particular are drawn to some of the fragrant aromas, but herbs like chamomile, foxglove, and common tobacco leaf can lead to paralysis, elevated heart rates, and even death in your pet.

For safety's sake, do your homework. Most of the spells in this book involve external use, such as in sachets, dressing candles, or stuffing poppets. If you're considering ingesting an herb or applying it to your skin, invest in a comprehensive herbal almanac. You'll find plenty of suggestions in the Resources and References sections. Familiarize yourself with the plants you use the most and their side effects; a field guide to your local herbs will come in handy.

Finally, remember herbs are often listed by folkloric names. Make sure you also study their scientific names and classifications. This will help you confirm whether what you're looking at and what you *think* you're looking at are the same plant.

The bottom line? Use caution and common sense, and if you're in any doubt about an herb's safety, don't use it.

Properties and Considerations

Magical herbs are living, breathing entities, each with their own unique characteristics. By getting to know the various plants you're working with and studying more than just traditional correspondences, you can build a relationship with them that will allow you to tap into their greatest potential for magic of every kind.

Just like people, herbs are affected by their environment. In the early 1970s, authors Peter Tompkins and Christopher Bird conducted a study in which plants were divided into two groups and treated differently; they later wrote about the results in *The Secret Life of Plants*. Half the plants were showered with words of kindness, and they thrived. The other half received hurtful language, and these plants withered and died. Herbs have energetic properties and vibrations that respond to the world around them, so consider your intention and how your herbs will absorb the energy you're putting out.

In addition to the common names for herbs, we'll cover folkloric names for the 40 different herbs we're discussing in part 2—for instance, mistletoe could be identified as Holy Wood, Devil's Fuge, or Witches' Broom, depending on where one lives. Because plants are often called by different things in different parts of the world, it's important to learn the Latin names as well—European mistletoe is always *Viscum album*, no matter where you might be. Herbal magic can be impacted by the plant's gender—yes, most plants are either masculine or feminine—as well as planetary and elemental influences. Ultimately, when you're working with magical herbs, be aware of these different factors, because they're all going to subtly—or not so subtly—impact the result of any spell you cast.

GENDER

Like people, plants have a gender. Although the terminology is rooted in fairly sexist stereotyping rather than science, the fact remains that we've come to associate particular plants with qualities that are traditionally seen as masculine or feminine.

Plants that have strong and powerful energy are viewed as masculine. These plants, such as mistletoe, basil, sage, and tobacco leaf, are used for protection, lust, courage, and banishing. Meanwhile, plants like apple blossom, mugwort, thyme, and vervain are viewed as feminine and associated with love, beauty, psychic powers, intuition, peace, and harmony.

Many modern practitioners have stopped using gender classifications because of the sexist overtones, and instead have begun referring to herbs as "hot" or "cold," or even "dry" and "wet." For the purposes of this book, we'll be using "masculine" and "feminine" for the sake of continuity with older, traditional texts.

MAGICAL INTENTIONS

When it comes to magical intentions, think of the different purposes you might have for working magic, herbal or otherwise. After all, to do magic is to bring about change. Nearly all magical workings fall into a few common categories.

Protection magic is a popular magical intention—after all, people have wanted to keep themselves safe since the first time one human encountered another. Protection spells can prevent physical attack, theft, or even negative energy.

Love magic is found around the world. Most magical belief systems caution against performing love workings toward specific people; instead, consider doing one to attract love, without selecting a named individual.

Healing magic can be traced back to early herbal medicine. It is used to ease pain and bring about physical and mental wellness. Use healing magic in tandem with professional healthcare, not as a substitute.

Money magic isn't going to make you a millionaire overnight, but prosperity workings can lower debt and bring extra cash your way.

Divinatory magic spells will help you tap into your greater wisdom, enhance your intuitive gifts, and exercise psychic clarity.

PLANETARY RULERS

In many forms of traditional magic, each herb is associated with a specific planetary ruler, which you'll learn more about in part 2. The planets themselves correspond to different types of magical workings based on the seven classical planets of the ancients. For instance, for workings related to protection or success in an upcoming court case, you might use herbs related to the sun. If your working is focused on dreams and intuition, work with a plant associated with the moon.

For spellwork connected to money and good old-fashioned luck, work with herbs that have Jupiter as their ruler. Venus, as you might imagine, is a soft and feminine planet, associated with love spells, beauty, and friendship. Mars, on the other hand, is connected to courage, lust, and sexual prowess and potency—it's a hyper-masculine sort of planet.

Herbs ruled by Saturn may work best for you to do some banishing, hex-breaking, or putting an end to something. For herbal magic related to divination and wisdom, work with herbs corresponding to the planet Mercury.

ELEMENTAL RULERS

Like the planets, each herb has an elemental ruler based upon the four classical elements—earth, air, fire, and water. Understanding these elements can help identify the right magical herbs for your workings.

The element of earth, corresponding to the north, is associated with money and prosperity as well as the security and stability of home life.

Consider herbs connected to air, the element associated with the east, for workings related to your own psychic and mental abilities, as well as prophetic visions and spiritual wisdom.

If your spellwork focuses on power and strength, including courage and protection, try tapping into the energies of herbs associated with fire, the southern element.

Finally, if you need to do a working related to purification, healing, love, friendship, or meditation, it's time to break out the water-ruled herbs, associated with the west.

COLORS

Colors, like planets and elements, have their own unique correspondences. Consider color correspondences for things like poppets, sachets, amulets, and oils, all of which we'll cover in chapter 3.

Red is associated with courage and power, as well as lust and passionate love. Use pink for workings focusing on emotional or spiritual healing, as well as friendship and pure, long-term love relationships. Purple is the color of power and ambition.

Orange is a great color to use for magic related to encouragement, attraction, and creativity. Work with gold for magic related to money, business, and overall financial abundance. Yellow is useful for protection, but it's also a color that brings happiness.

Green is associated with money magic and fertility; use it to facilitate forgiveness and compassion, as well as love and empathy. A light, baby blue can bring about good health and overall wellness, while dark blue can help us connect to our psychic skills and ability to let go of emotional baggage.

Black is associated with banishing, while white is tied to purity, truth, and the power of the divine.

Enchantment

You may wish to enchant your herbs prior to use, to let your herbs know what their magical purpose is and increase their effectiveness. Many people find it works best if they enchant their herbs right before using them for magic.

To enchant fresh or dried herbs, place them at your workspace between candles of a color that aligns with your magical intention. For instance, for a working for love using apple blossoms, you might light a pair of pink or red candles. Light the candles, hold the herb in your hands, and say, *Apple blossom, guided by Venus and the powers of water, I task you with bringing love into my life.* As you say these words, visualize the plant filling up with loving energy, or whatever sort of energy is appropriate for your magical intention. In his *Encyclopedia of Magical Herbs,* author Scott Cunningham points out that you can even sing or chant to your herbs to enchant them. If you'll be working with multiple herbs—for example, to make an incense blend—you can put each into a ceramic or wooden bowl together as you enchant them individually.

Attunement

Some practitioners do an attunement with their herbs in addition to, or instead of, enchantment. This is a process by which the practitioner becomes familiar with the energy vibrations of the plant, and there are several methods you can use. Again, you should wait to do this until right before you perform your working for maximum magical efficiency.

For a simple attunement, place your herb in a bowl. Place your dominant hand in the bowl, running your fingers gently through the loose leaves of the herb. Close your eyes. Imagine the energy from that plant emanating out of the leaves and filling you with its vibrations. Can you feel love radiating from the herb? Power? Protective energy? Feel the magic coming from the plant and visualize the process by which you will incorporate it into your spellwork. When you have finished and can see the magical energy in the plant, be sure to thank your herbs before moving on.

SELF-LOVE BATH BOMB BAG
page 109

ꝑRACTICING ꝳAGIC

Now that you know how magical herbs work and what to consider when selecting them, let's get down to the key factors of magical practice. Be aware that magical herbalism isn't restricted to any single spiritual group—no matter what your religious beliefs may be, you can practice magical herbalism. Herbs don't care which god or goddess—if any—you honor.

We're going to explore some of the common spells, rituals, and herbal preparations you'll encounter in part 3 of this book. In addition, you'll learn about some of the essential tools to be found in any magical herbalist's pantry; after all, a well-stocked kitchen is a wonderful place to make magic!

The Magical Use of Herbs

In every place humans have settled, there has been documented use of herbal knowledge. Herbs—including the flowers, bark, roots, stems, and leaves—are also the mainstay of curative practice for shamans, medicine men, village healers, and witches all over the world.

For centuries, magical and healing herbal lore was passed down as oral tradition from one generation to the next. As people began developing written language, they recorded this magical herbal knowledge in some of the world's oldest written texts. The Greek Magical Papyri, written between 100 BCE and 400 CE, contain herbal spells, rituals, and formulas. Some medical books of the medieval period contained herbal remedies that modern readers might consider spellwork. The Nine Herbs Charm, found in a collection of tenth century Anglo-Saxon medical texts called the *Lacnunga,* gives an herbal blend for treating poisoning and infections in the form of a poem, including instructions to sing the charm during application.

Like other living things, herbs carry vibrational energies. They can be used independently in spellwork or to enhance a working already in progress. Herbs can be consumed as teas, used in a bath or as a floor wash, stuffed dry into poppets, or burned as incense to release their smoke into the universe. To select herbs for your magical purposes, begin by consulting part 2 of this book, which includes 40 different magical herbs and their correspondences, and then review the spells contained in part 3. When you are ready to expand your knowledge even further, delve into the reading lists in the Resources and References sections, which include several comprehensive herbal guides.

Types of Spells, Rituals, and Preparations

There are numerous easy ways to use your herbs in spellwork. The method you choose will depend on your purpose, as well as the resources available to you. You may discover that you prefer one type of spell or preparation over the others. Perhaps you love sewing poppets, or maybe you really enjoy blending herbal bath mixtures. Find what you like and develop your skill in that area.

SACHETS & PILLOWS

Herbal sachets and pillows are easy to make, and they're a great way to use up scrap fabric. A sachet is simply a small cloth bag stuffed with aromatic flowers and herbs, and then tied or sewn shut. You can also buy tulle or muslin drawstring bags at your local craft store.

To make your own herbal sachet or pillow, use a breathable fabric like linen or lightweight cotton. Cut two pieces of fabric of equal size—three to five inches is a good guideline—and stitch them along the edges, right sides together, on three sides. Turn your bag right side out, and stuff your magical herbs through the open end. Stitch the fourth side closed, or simply gather the opening together and use a bit of decorative ribbon or twine to tie it shut.

Place herbal sachets in your dresser drawers to give your clothing a magical scent, use them in ritual baths, carry them in your pocket, or tuck them under your pillow so you can inhale their fragrances as you sleep. Use spells like the Protection Pouch Sachet Spell (page 89) or the Soothing Sachet (page 117) to get started making sachets and pillows.

HERBAL PENDULUMS

Have you ever had a question where the answer had to be binary in nature? It was either a *Yes* or *No*, or perhaps *Go* or *Stay*. Maybe it was a choice between two people or two places. Regardless, this sort of divination is where pendulum magic comes in handy.

Ideally, to make a pendulum, you'll need something with a bit of weight to it. Most herbs are fairly light, but there are a couple of options. You can use something heavier, such as a cinnamon stick or a Buckeye nut, or you can use a piece of wood, as seen in the Herbal Pendulum Magic spell (page 153). Another option is to gather a teaspoon of herbs and place them with a small stone in a small square of cloth. Gather the corners together, twist the cloth, and tie it shut with a bit of string.

Attach your weight to a chain or string about 14 inches long. To calibrate your pendulum, hold it steady and ask a question to which you know the answer will be *Yes*. Whichever way it swings is your *Yes* direction. Now ask a question that you know must be answered as a *No*. Once you understand which way your pendulum goes for *Yes* and *No*, you can ask divinatory questions to figure out the outcome.

AMULETS

Amulets, sometimes called charms or talismans, may be the oldest form of known herbal magic, dating back thousands of years. An amulet is any sort of natural object that has been consecrated and then used for magical purposes. Consecration is the process of cleansing an item of any past energy or influences for ritual and magical use. Over the centuries, people have used everything from pieces of wood and animal bones to stones with holes in them or large seeds like acorns or chestnuts.

Amulets are a useful sort of magic for healing and protective workings, and they're easy to make. An amulet is something you can carry in your pocket, such as the Pocket Love Charm (page 105), or wear as a necklace, such as the Psychic Amulet (page 145). By choosing plants that correspond with your magical intention, you can create an amulet out of any herb.

The easiest method for making an herbal amulet is to create a small drawstring bag and add the appropriate herbs, stones, and other items to it. Once it's made and closed up, an amulet bag should not be opened until the magical goal has been met.

POPPETS

A poppet is one of the easiest forms of sympathetic magic. A poppet is a magical doll that can be used for all kinds of magical intentions. If you need love in your life, try the Love Poppets (page 105), or stitch up some healing magic with the Happy Healthy Whole Poppet (page 123).

The way a poppet works is simple: The doll is a substitute for the person who is the target of the magical working, whether it's you or someone else. To make a basic poppet, cut two pieces of fabric in the shape of a person, like a gingerbread man. Sew around the edges, but leave an opening. Stuff it with filling and herbs, as well as a magical link to identify who the poppet represents. This can be a piece of hair or clothing, a photo, or even a piece of paper with the person's name on it that you stuff inside the doll. Sew it closed. Once you've created a poppet, consecrate it—be sure to enchant it first, telling it what its ultimate magical purpose will be.

INFUSIONS

Infusions are created by steeping herbs in water. Unlike teas or tisanes, which are primarily made from steeping only leaves, an infusion is often brewed with the leaves, stems, roots, and flowers of a plant. While they are not something you should create with every plant in your collection—after all, some aren't safe to be taken internally—infusions are a great way to take advantage of an herb's rich flavors. Many medicinal herbs are used in infusions to treat a variety of ailments; they can be consumed either warm or cold, or they can be incorporated into salves and ointments for topical use. Before consuming any herbal infusion internally, however, be sure to check with your healthcare professional to make sure there are no contra-indications for you.

To make your own herbal infusions, like the Healing Water Hand Wash (page 120), simply place a tablespoon of the dried herb of your choice into a glass jar with a lid. Add a cup of boiling water, seal the lid, and allow the herbs to steep for at least eight hours. Strain the herbs out of the water by pouring through cheesecloth, and discard the used herbs. The leftover liquid is your infusion.

BATHS

A magical herbal bath is a powerful way to use your herbs. Ritual baths are found in a number of spiritual traditions around the world and can allow you to absorb the power and energy of the plant throughout your entire body; these are especially effective for healing magic and purifica-tion spells. You can make an herbal bath blend by combining your dried herbs in a bowl, mixing them up, and then scooping them into a muslin or cheesecloth bag. Hang the bag over the end of your tub's faucet, so the warm water courses directly over your herbs—you'll get a chance to make one of these with the Self-Love Bath Bomb Bag (page 109).

Another way to take an herbal bath is to add an infusion directly into your bathwater, as you'll do with the Spiritual Bath Blend (page 147). You may even want to try using essential oils of the appropriate herbs, adding a few drops to your water. Be sure the oils are properly diluted. Use too much, and you'll end up with an unpleasant skin irritation.

POTIONS

When we refer to a magical potion, we typically mean something that can be consumed in liquid form such as a tea, infusion, decoction, or other preparation. Do your due diligence when it comes to magical herbs that you might be planning on drinking; be sure to only ingest herbs that are known to be safe for human consumption, such as those in your kitchen pantry.

In addition to brewing up an herbal infusion, you may want to turn some of your herbs into a potion by way of drinkable tea; it's similar to an infusion, but the preparation method is slightly different. To brew a tea, such as Vervain Water (page 97), add a small amount of your dried herbs to a tea ball or bag, and begin steeping them in a pot of water before it reaches full boil. After it's boiling, remove the pot from the heat and allow the herbs to steep another ten minutes. Remove the tea bag or ball and pour the water into a cup to drink hot, or refrigerate it for an hour to make a cold tea.

LOTIONS & OINTMENTS

Ointments and salves are a fantastic delivery method for herbal magic. These are easy to make, and can be created by mixing dried, powdered herbs into a fatty substance like shortening or even beeswax. Select a magical herb that suits your purpose, and use your mortar and pestle to grind ¼ cup of it into a powder. Blend the herbs into a cup of your base, and store it in an airtight container, ideally a dark-colored glass or ceramic jar with a lid. Be sure to use this blend within six months.

You can also heat the shortening or wax in a double boiler on your stove, and then add the powdered herbs. Let your mixture cool, and then store it. To use an ointment or salve, like the Get the Jump on the Job Salve (page 139), apply a small amount to your pulse points, or use it to moisturize appropriate body parts like the backs of your hands, your elbows, or your feet.

Lotions work in a similar fashion and can be applied to most of your body. To make an herbal lotion, combine ⅓ cup jojoba or almond oil, ¼ cup coconut oil, and ¼ cup softened or melted beeswax in a bowl. Stir them until blended, and then mix in essential oils from the herbs that are appropriate to your magical purpose. Store it in a dark-colored glass or ceramic bottle with an airtight cap.

OILS

Making your own essential oils is labor intensive and cost prohibitive for most people. Instead, you can source them from a variety of reputable places.

To blend a magical oil, use ¼ cup of an unscented base such as jojoba, almond, grapeseed, or safflower oil. Using a dropper, add very small amounts of the essential oils serving your purpose, and then mix by swirling, rather than stirring. In traditional aromatherapy, swirling gives you an idea of the final scent; in magic, it prevents you from introducing foreign material into your oil blend. Store your oil blends in dark-colored glass bottles away from heat and moisture, and use within six months. Amy Blackthorn, author of *Blackthorn's Botanical Magic*, recommends checking the shelf life of your carrier oil; she suggests putting an expiration date on the label for any oils, so they don't go rancid before use.

Oil blends can be used in a number of ways. Use them to anoint a candle, as with the Moonlight Divination Candle spell (page 150). Anointing is lightly coating the candle with oil while enchanting it with your magical intent. Dab oils on inanimate objects, as you'll do with the Protection Oil (page 89), or on your own skin—as long as they're properly diluted to avoid irritation.

Note that even though many commercially available oils are synthetic to keep costs down, most practitioners of magic agree that they are still effective in spellwork.

INCENSE

Blending your own loose-leaf incense using dried herbs is an especially effective way of attaining magical goals. Once you've combined your plant materials, simply burn them or allow them to sit on a charcoal disc and smolder. To do this, take a disc—they're available in nearly every spiritual shop—and place it in a fire-safe bowl or cauldron. Light the disc and allow it to heat up; once you start seeing small sparks along the outside, it's ready. Gently place your loose-leaf incense blend on top of the disc, and it will smolder and burn.

You can use incense in different ways: It can be a part of the spell itself, as you'll see with the Lavender Love Incense (page 103) and the Inspirational Intuition Incense Blend (page 149). Alternatively, you can use it as an enhancement for other workings and simply have it burning in the background to heighten the magical energy with its vibrations.

SPELLS

In addition to all of the other magical preparations you can use for herbal magic, there are times when you'll use herbs simply as part of a spell. No infusion, no stuffing them into a poppet, just plain old spellwork. In these cases, the herb will often represent a concept, an action, or a goal. For instance, in the Healing Wreath for the Sickroom (page 124), the herbs are simply utilized at their most basic level to bring their healing energies into a space where they are most needed. Likewise, the Herbal Braid (page 91) is merely a braid of herbs, and it is their own natural vibrations that matter most in the spell, not the manner in which they are prepared.

Can you do spells other than the ones you'll find in this book? Absolutely! Once you've selected your herbs, it's only a matter of figuring out *how* to use them—and you can write your own spell by formally declaring your will and intent.

The Magic Herbalist's Pantry

Before you begin practicing magical herbalism, there are a few items you should gather in advance, so that everything you need will be right at your fingertips. Be sure that all of your jars, bags, and bottles are properly labeled and stored where they won't be exposed to direct sunlight or extreme temperatures.

HERBS

The key to practicing herb magic is having on hand the herbs you use the most. Although the 40 different herbs covered in part 2 of this book cover a variety of magical purposes, you don't need to have all of them in stock all the time. Select a few you think you'll use the most as the basis of your herbal collection; you may find it useful to acquire commonly used plants like basil, rosemary, lavender, patchouli, and sage, and build your inventory from there. Keep them in your pantry or grow them in your garden.

TOOLS

Although there are many magical tools used in herbal spellwork, most of the spells and rituals in this book use the following:

Mortar and Pestle: Use your mortar and pestle to grind and crush your dried herbs into powder.

Bowls: Use bowls for blending herbal mixes.

Jars: Store herbs in jars with tight-fitting lids. Jars made of dark glass are ideal.

Candles: Many spells call for candles, so keep them on hand in a variety of sizes, shapes, and colors.

Cauldron: Use a small cast-iron cauldron to burn your herbs on a charcoal disc. Some practitioners like to use a censer instead.

Charcoal Discs: These can be used to burn your loose incense blends and can be purchased in packages at just about any spiritual supply store.

Knife: In many magical traditions, a special knife called a boline is used to cut fresh herbs. Traditionally, it's made with a wooden handle and a curved blade, but you can use any knife you've consecrated. Make sure you only use this knife for magical purposes.

Unscented Oil: This will come in handy as a base or carrier for your herbs and can also be used to anoint candles. Use jojoba, almond, grapeseed, or safflower oil—some practitioners prefer extra-virgin olive oil.

OTHER INGREDIENTS

There are a few other items you may find useful for the spells in this book.

Fabric, Needles, and Thread: Use these for making sachets and pillows, as well as sewing magical poppets.

Ribbon, String, or Leather Cording: Plan on using these when you're creating amulets, talismans, and charm bags to be worn around the neck or hung up in the home.

Paper: Many spells involve the writing of intentions, goals, and even names. Use nice paper in your magic—ideally, something that feels special to you works best.

Ink Pen: Have a good ink pen on hand that you use for magical purposes only. Some people like to use a quill or feather pen with a bottle of ink in a color that relates to their magical intent.

~ PART TWO ~

MAGIC HERBS

Today, practitioners incorporate just about every known herb into spells and rituals. The herbs included in this section can be found in your local metaphysical shop or botanica, or you can order them online from reputable vendors. There are a couple listed in the back of this book.

When you're working with magic herbs, they should be treated as sacred. Don't toss them in a pile with a bunch of junk on your desk when you're finished; show them the respect that they deserve. The better you honor the plants you work with, the better your magical results will be.

PEACEFUL PROTECTION POTTED PLANT
page 96

CHAPTER

4

ƑORTY ℳAGIC ℋERBS

Are you ready to get started using herbs in magic and spellwork? This chapter will introduce you to 40 of the common magical herbs used for the spells in part 3 of this book, a solid foundation upon which you can build your magical studies. Remember, if you're doing healing magic, herbal spells should be used in tandem with treatment from an appropriate medical or mental health professional.

Each entry in this book includes an illustration of the herb, Latin and folkloric names, and correspondences. You'll learn about planetary and elemental rulers, gender, and perhaps most important, how to use each herb in magic. Ideally, you should take the time to get to know an herb before you use it. Touch it, crush the leaves between your fingertips to release the fragrances, inhale their aromas. Learn about the herb and form a connection to it—and then you'll be ready to use it in magic.

Allspice ....

- **Common Name:** Allspice
- **Latin Name:** *Pimenta officinalis*
- **Folk Name:** Clove pepper, Jamaica pepper, pimento
- **Gender:** Masculine
- **Magical Purpose:** Money, luck, revitalization
- **Planetary Ruler:** Mars
- **Elemental Ruler:** Fire

If you do any baking, you likely have allspice in your pantry, making it ideal for spellwork around the house. It tastes like a combination of cloves, cinnamon, and pepper, and is indigenous to the West Indies and South America. Thanks to its delightful smell, it can be incorporated in incense blends to attract money and good fortune.

Allspice has been used for medicinal applications in the past; it's considered an aromatic stimulant and was utilized as a flavoring additive blended into tonics that cured digestive disorders. In some places, the berries were boiled down, reduced to a paste, and integrated into poultices that aided in the treatment of rheumatic aches and pains.

MAGICAL USES: For healing magic, use allspice in the Soothing Sachet spell (page 117). Mix allspice into other incense blends to make them smell magical, and then burn them for overall healing in your home. Keep a bowl of fragrant allspice in a place of prominence in your house to attract luck.

To boost your cash flow, incorporate some allspice into your magic with the Moneybags Money Bag (page 131), Wealth Wash for Your Home (page 138), and Spread the Wealth Money Oil (page 140). Sprinkle allspice into your wallet or purse to give your finances a boost. If you own a business, place allspice near the cash register and customers will be drawn to spend more money with you—plus they'll be complimentary about how wonderful your shop or office smells!

Aloe ....

- **Common Name:** Aloe
- **Latin Name:** *Aloe vera*
- **Folk Name:** Burn plant, sea houseleek, first aid plant
- **Gender:** Feminine
- **Magical Purpose:** Protection, healing, relief of loneliness, attracting love
- **Planetary Ruler:** Venus
- **Elemental Ruler:** Water

Aloe has short, stubby stems with thick, fleshy green offsets. Although it's technically an evergreen perennial, it's a beautiful succulent that's pretty hard to kill and primarily appears in temperate and tropical regions, including parts of the Middle East and northern Africa. By the eighteenth century, it was in China and the Americas.

Anyone who's experienced pain from a sunburn is familiar with aloe's cooling properties on the skin, but it can be used to treat other conditions, including lacerations and blisters. In fact, it's so skin-friendly that it's an ingredient in many hygiene products as a moisturizer, including shaving cream and sunscreen. The juices, which can be squeezed out through the fat ends of the leaves, are helpful for relief of constipation and colitis; a 2018 study by researchers Seung Wook Hong, Jaeyoung Chun, and Hyun Jung Lee confirmed it's an effective and safe treatment for irritable bowel syndrome and other digestive disorders.

MAGICAL USES: When it comes to magic, aloe has a lot of potential! It's often associated with protection, so why not plant some in pretty pots around your home? This is said to keep negative energy away from your house, as well as protect your family from unfortunate household accidents. In some magical traditions, aloe is associated with the relief of loneliness; if you're feeling blue, keep a well-watered aloe plant nearby to lift your spirits. Give your plant a name, assign it a job in your home—keeping you company—and talk to it regularly.

Use fresh aloe for healing by enchanting the leaves, breaking them open, and rubbing the juices on a poppet or doll, or in the Healing Water Hand Wash (page 120) and Happy Healthy Whole Poppet (page 123) spells. In some forms of folk magic, aloe is used to settle restless ghosts; plant aloe on top of a grave to bring peace to the deceased person in the afterlife. Because of its association with Venus and water, use dried aloe leaves, burned at the time of the waxing or full moon, to bring love into your life. Incorporate it into beauty spells: Add the gel-like juices to your favorite face wash as a moisturizer, and dab it onto your face, visualizing yourself becoming more lovely, both inside and out.

Apple Blossom ....

- **Common Name:** Apple
- **Latin Name:** *Malus domestica*
- **Folk Name:** Fruit of the gods, silver branch, tree of love
- **Gender:** Feminine
- **Magical Purpose:** Healing, love and beauty, money
- **Planetary Ruler:** Venus
- **Elemental Ruler:** Water

There are hundreds of varieties of apple trees cultivated around the world, and while the fruits themselves have magical applications—and taste fantastic!—the blossoms also have value in spiritual practice. Apples are associated with the divine work of the gods, as well as death, the underworld, and immortality. In some folkloric traditions, apples serve as a gateway to the world of the faerie realm.

Apples are full of malic and tartaric acids, which are helpful in medicinal uses. That old saying about an apple a day keeping the doctor away isn't wrong; early healers knew prescribing apples as a regular part of the diet helped prevent a number of maladies. The blossoms themselves can be brewed into an infusion and added to baths or washes for healing, love, beauty, and divination.

MAGICAL USES: Apples are associated with abundance and prosperity. To bring bounty into your life, hang garlands of apple blossoms around your home, particularly over your bed if you're trying to conceive. The apple blossom is great for love magic—try the Apple Blossom Countdown spell (page 107). Brew the flowers into an infusion and use it to wash your face and hair if you want to feel beautiful and attract romance.

To invite healing magic into your life, mix apple blossoms into a batch of the Healing Incense Blend (page 117). For some money magic, fire up the Penny Power spell (page 135) or the Beeswax Money Candle (page 137). Use these fragrant little flowers for divination by burning them as incense when you're trying to do spirit work, readings, or scrying. If you've got an entire apple, use it in love divination by peeling it in a continuous length; when the first strip of peel falls off, it will form the initial of your future lover's name. Cut your apple in half and count the seeds; an even number means romance is on the way, but an uneven number means you'll probably stay single for a while.

Basil ....

- ⚬ **Common Name:** Basil
- ⚬ **Latin Name:** *Ocimum basilicum*
- ⚬ **Folk Name:** St. Joseph's wort, albahaca, witches' herb
- ⚬ **Gender:** Masculine
- ⚬ **Magical Purpose:** Divination and spirit work, love, protection
- ⚬ **Planetary Ruler:** Mars
- ⚬ **Elemental Ruler:** Fire

Found in culinary creations around the world, fragrant basil is one herb you probably have in your kitchen's spice rack already. There are a number of varieties, including common or sweet basil, all of which are useful in magic. The Greeks associated basil with misfortune and poverty, but the Romans saw it as an herb that grew and flourished the more it was mistreated. In Mediterranean countries, where basil appears in savory dishes, it is also strewn on floors to purify a home. The gift of a potted basil plant guarantees good fortune if you present it to friends moving into a new house.

It's said basil can bring peace and friendship between enemies and is often associated with love magic. In some countries, however, basil is considered a womanly herb that real men don't consume, because healers of the past have used it to make teas that provide relief from painful menstrual periods. **Avoid using basil essential oil during pregnancy.**

MAGICAL USES: Basil is super useful for protection—try the Basil Bath Bag (page 91). Plant it around your property to keep enemies away, or crush the fresh leaves and scatter them around your house to eliminate negative energies. Burn dried basil in your incense blends to prevent malevolent spirits from taking up residence.

If you want to boost your love life, try Hey Baby Basil Magic (page 112). Basil can also be used to detect fidelity: Place a fresh leaf on your lover's hand, and if it wilts there's a chance they've been unfaithful. To keep your partner loyal, sprinkle dried and powdered basil in the bed while they sleep. Divination workings are a great time to break out your basil leaves—try the Basil Wisdom spell (page 146) and the Awakening Oil (page 154).

Bay Leaf ....

- ○ **Common Name:** Bay
- ○ **Latin Name:** *Laurus nobilis*
- ○ **Folk Name:** Roman laurel, sweet bay, bay laurel, laurel of Apollo
- ○ **Gender:** Masculine
- ○ **Magical Purpose:** Protection and strength, healing, purification, exorcism
- ○ **Planetary Ruler:** Sun
- ○ **Elemental Ruler:** Fire

Originating in Asia and then spreading via the Mediterranean to the rest of the world, the bay leaf is used as a flavoring in savory meals and has both medicinal and magical applications. In ancient Greece, the oracle at Delphi chewed bay leaves and inhaled smoke from the burning leaves to bring about prophetic visions. Bay was popular in the Roman world as well; emperors and heroes were often crowned with a wreath of bay laurel.

In the Middle Ages, bay was used by healers to treat maladies like fungal and bacterial infections, headaches, and digestive discomfort. It was also brewed into a strong tea and mixed with other abortifacient herbs to stimulate uterine contractions. **Do not ingest bay leaf if you are pregnant or breastfeeding.**

MAGICAL USES: Bay leaf is wonderful for protection magic—try the Home Purification Wash for Floors & Doors (page 93) or the Magical Mayhem Jar Spell (page 98). Fold some bay leaves into a sachet and carry it as an amulet to keep negative energy away. Mix dried bay with sandalwood and burn it as incense if you think someone might be planning to fling a curse or hex your way.

For healing magic, include bay leaf in the Get Better Bath Spell (page 123). Add bay to consecrated water and sprinkle it around a sickroom, or use it as a hand and face wash for overall healing. Bay is also said to promote strength; if you're involved in physical activities, tuck a bay leaf in each shoe for extra stamina, like athletes and wrestlers did in the ancient world. Is there someone from your past you'd like to hear from? Write their name on a bay leaf, and tuck it in your phone case to attract a call or message.

Bergamot ....

- **Common Name:** Bergamot
- **Latin Name:** *Monarda didyma*
- **Folk Name:** Bee balm, orange mint, horsemint
- **Gender:** Masculine
- **Magical Purpose:** Prosperity, protection and hex-breaking, healing
- **Planetary Ruler:** Mercury
- **Elemental Ruler:** Air

Like many herbs we use today, bergamot is native to North America. It's a perennial, often grown as an ornamental, with a floral and slightly citrusy fragrance. The Oswego people brewed the leaves into a tea which became popular with American colonists boycotting British tea shipments. Native American groups in the Mid-Atlantic region used four different varieties of bergamot in both medicine and ceremonies. There's also the bergamot orange, originating in the Middle East and northern Africa, which traveled to North America with enslaved peoples during the early colonial period.

Bergamot gained popularity in Europe for holistic treatment of gastric disorders. According to Maud Grieve's *A Modern Herbal*, early practitioners boiled it into tea to relieve upset stomachs and diarrhea. It also came in handy to lower fevers, soothe colicky babies, and alleviate menstrual discomfort.

MAGICAL USES: Use bergamot for protection against magical attack, particularly the breaking of a hex or curse. If you're the recipient of magical malfeasance, add bergamot into your bath water, take a good long soak, and allow the bergamot to draw the curse away, sending it down the drain when you let the water out of the bathtub. Be cautious if using the essential oil of the bergamot plant; it can cause burns or blisters on the skin if it isn't properly diluted. Use bergamot in the Purification Incense Blend (page 94). Bergamot's natural medicinal properties make it a great herb for healing magic as well. Use a mortar and pestle to grind the stems, leaves, and flowers into a powder, and anoint a candle for health and wellness spells.

Bergamot is typically associated with magic related to wealth and financial success. Sprinkle loose bergamot into your wallet or a coin jar, or dab a bit of the oil on folded paper cash; it will attract more money to what you already have. Blend dried bergamot with other money-drawing herbs and plants and burn it on a charcoal disc as loose incense, or scoop it into a sachet and carry it with you for financial luck. Use bergamot in the Moneybags Money Bag (page 131), the Bountiful Blessings Incense (page 136), and the Spread the Wealth Money Oil (page 140).

Black Cohosh ....

- **Common Name:** Black cohosh
- **Latin Name:** *Actaea racemosa*
- **Folk Name:** Black bugbane, black snake root
- **Gender:** Masculine
- **Magical Purpose:** Ward off evil, home protection, curse-breaking, women's mysteries
- **Planetary Ruler:** Pluto
- **Elemental Ruler:** Fire

Black cohosh is indigenous to the eastern half of the United States and typically grows in woody areas. It has large compound leaves and white, tiny-clustered flowers appearing in late spring and early summer. It has a somewhat unpleasant smell—this aroma actually helps keep bugs away, so it's become popular as an ornamental in suburban gardens.

Some Native American healers used black cohosh to treat kidney disorders, malaria, and even plain old coughs and colds. Its most popular medical use, though, is in the care of menstrual discomfort, including hot flashes and night sweats; English physician Nicholas Culpeper recommended it in his *Complete Herbal.* Because black cohosh can cause the cervix to dilate, there is a risk of miscarriage. **Avoid handling black cohosh essential oil during pregnancy.**

MAGICAL USES: Worried about magical attack? Plant black cohosh around the doors of your home or sprinkle the dried leaves on your thresholds to keep evil away. Brew a decoction by steeping the leaves in boiling water; once it cools, use it to wash your floors or walls for magical self-defense around the house. If you're worried you might be under the influence of a curse, stuff the leaves or dried roots of black cohosh into a protective poppet to repel hostile magic. Use black cohosh in the Protection Pouch Sachet Spell (page 89) and the Spell to Stop a Gossip (page 98).

For love magic, try the Pocket Love Charm (page 105). Got an unwanted suitor? Mix black cohosh with rose petals, mash them together, and dab the secretions on your pulse points to get rid of them; they'll stay far away. If you're having a tough time during your menstrual period, use the Spell to Soothe a Savage Cycle (page 119). Carry a piece of the root in your pocket or in a sachet to repel unexpected illness.

Buckeye ....

- **Common Name:** Buckeye
- **Latin Name:** *Aesculus glabra*
- **Folk Name:** Conker, horse chestnut
- **Gender:** Masculine
- **Magical Purpose:** Money, luck, healing
- **Planetary Ruler:** Jupiter
- **Elemental Ruler:** Fire

The buckeye, commonly called the horse chestnut, is the seed of a large deciduous tree found in the American Midwest and plains regions, and parts of Canada. Native American tribes in these areas often blanched freshly harvested buckeyes and used the tannic acid to process deer hide. It isn't without its medicinal purposes; the bark and nuts were sometimes made into a poultice or decoction to treat rheumatism. The buckeye found its way to the South along trade routes, and soon became a symbol of gambler's luck.

The buckeye tree has thin leaves growing in clusters of five, and the seeds, or nuts, grow inside a firm outer shell with a spiny covering. Unless you're a squirrel, **the buckeye is poisonous**, so keep them out of reach of pets and children.

MAGICAL USES: Buckeyes are associated with good fortune at the gaming tables, so if you're a gambler, carry one in your pocket and rub it between the fingers of your dominant hand before you roll the dice or hit the slot machines. Drill a hole in a dried one and wear it on a cord around your neck to ensure financial success. Bring even more money your way with a buckeye when you use the Plant a Money Tree spell (page 132).

The buckeye also has healing properties, particularly if you're suffering from gout, rheumatism, or neurological complaints. Tuck them under your mattress at points corresponding to your aches and pains to alleviate symptoms.

Catnip

- **Common Name:** Catnip
- **Latin Name:** *Nepeta cataria*
- **Folk Name:** Cat mint, field balm, cat wort
- **Gender:** Feminine
- **Magical Purpose:** Cleansing and purification, love and beauty, happiness
- **Planetary Ruler:** Venus
- **Elemental Ruler:** Water

If you've ever had the pleasure of sharing your home with a feline friend, you know catnip is a magical herb indeed! In addition to sending your cat into throes of ecstasy, the heart-shaped, aromatic leaves of the catnip plant were often blended into teas by physicians of the past and used to treat coughs and fever. Catnip is a perennial that grows just about everywhere in the world.

In China and Europe, early practitioners used catnip in ointments to treat skin conditions. It also became popular for its calming properties, and there are many legends of people self-medicating with catnip, although the delivery method is unspecified. In an interesting paradox, it's said chewing the roots can make people fierce and aggressive.

MAGICAL USES: It should be obvious, but catnip can help you bond with your cat—not just physically, but psychically. Sprinkle dried leaves in your cat's favorite spot and sit quietly to watch them enjoy it. Use catnip in your protection spells—make the Purification Incense Blend or Protection Oil (page 89). Grow it in pots near your door or windows to attract positive energy; watch out, though, as neighborhood cats might decide you're trying to attract *them*, too.

For health and wellness, brew an infusion of catnip and, once cool, use it as a hand or face wash. Catnip can be incorporated into love and beauty spells too, to enhance the way you appear to others. Try the Cool Cat Love Sachet (page 103), or combine it with other love-related herbs to burn as incense on a charcoal disc.

Chamomile ....

- **Common Name:** Chamomile
- **Latin Name:** *Anthemis nobilis*
- **Folk Name:** Ground apple, whig plant, maythen
- **Gender:** Masculine
- **Magical Purpose:** Money and luck, cleansing and purification, healing
- **Planetary Ruler:** Sun
- **Elemental Ruler:** Water

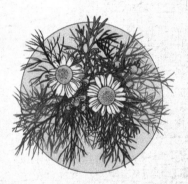

Chamomile, in its many varieties, has been popular in ornamental and medicinal gardens throughout history. The light yellow and white flowers look like tiny daisies and have an apple-like aroma that attracts bees and butterflies. During the Middle Ages, city dwellers in Europe used it as a fragrant strewing herb; when it was walked upon, the fresh scent was released, providing relief from the offensive odors found in urban areas of the time.

The whole plant has medicinal applications, but the flowers seem to be most beneficial. Brewed into a tea, chamomile treats everything from colds and coughs to anxiety. An infusion of chamomile was historically prescribed to relieve symptoms of digestive disorders. **Avoid using chamomile essential oil during pregnancy.**

MAGICAL USES: Use chamomile for protection with the Herbal Braid (page 91), Protective Wreath to Guard Your Door (page 92), and Safe & Secure Smudge Sticks (page 93). Plant chamomile around your home to keep trespassers away. If you suffer from nightmares, keep fresh chamomile under your pillow or in a vase beside your bed.

Incorporate chamomile into magic for overall wellness with the Healing Incense Blend (page 117). Don't overlook it for money magic— make a Prosperity Pocket Charm (page 133) or Beeswax Money Candle (page 137). Brew it into an infusion and use it to wash your hands before visiting the casino, or tuck the flowers into your wallet or purse to increase the money you've already got.

Cinnamon ....

- ❋ **Common Name:** Cinnamon
- ❋ **Latin Name:**
  Cinnamomum zeylandicum
- ❋ **Folk Name:** Sweet wood
- ❋ **Gender:** Masculine
- ❋ **Magical Purpose:** Intuition and psychic abilities, love and passion
- ❋ **Planetary Ruler:** Sun
- ❋ **Elemental Ruler:** Fire

Cinnamon has an unmistakable fragrance, and the dried bark is used in baking around the world. Although it's primarily exported from the Bahamas today, true cinnamon originates in Sri Lanka. Cinnamon has been used for millennia. The Egyptians used cinnamon oil as a perfume in embalming rituals, and during medieval times, physicians recommended the addition of cinnamon to medicines to treat throat ailments, congestion, and coughs. It gained popularity for preservative qualities once people discovered that cinnamon inhibits bacteria growth in meat, reducing spoilage. **Avoid using cinnamon essential oil during pregnancy.**

MAGICAL USES: Add cinnamon oil to a carrier oil to dilute it, and dab it on your pulse points for protection from hexes, curses, and those who would cause harm. Burn cinnamon sticks to cleanse your sacred space and pass your magical tools through the smoke to consecrate them. Cinnamon is a great enhancer for love magic! Try the Kiss Me Mouthwash Magic spell (page 104) and the Love Poppets (page 105) to put some sizzle in your romance.

Sprinkle cinnamon in your wallet or purse to draw good fortune, or carry a cinnamon stick in your pocket to attract extra cash. For divination workings, use cinnamon in the Psychic Amulet (page 145) and the Inspirational Intuition Incense Blend (page 149). In many magical traditions, it's believed that cinnamon raises your metaphysical vibration; you can also add it to any incense blend for a magical boost.

Cinquefoil ....

- **Common Name:** Cinquefoil
- **Latin Name:** *Potentilla canadensis*
- **Folk Name:** Five finger blossom, crampweed, silverweed, goose grass, five-leaf grass
- **Gender:** Masculine
- **Magical Purpose:** Dreams and prophecy, money, protection
- **Planetary Ruler:** Jupiter
- **Elemental Ruler:** Fire

A creeping plant with large yellow flowers, cinquefoil has leaflets that appear to be split into five separate points. The leaves and root found favor with early physicians as a treatment for fevers, especially those caused by the diseases carried in communal water supplies, such as dysentery and cholera.

The cinquefoil root was said to be beneficial when mashed into a paste and applied to the skin as a cure for achy joints. Growing in most parts of Europe and North America, this perennial was also a popular plant for love divination.

MAGICAL USES: Cinquefoil has plenty of protective properties, particularly against theft. Use it in the Keep Your Car Covered Protection Charm (page 95). Carry it in your pocket, and the five leaves of the cinquefoil will prevent hexes and curses. If you're fortunate enough to find a cinquefoil with seven leaves rather than five, placing it under your pillow will bring dreams of your future lover.

For a financial pick-me-up, use cinquefoil in the Cool Coin Purse (page 134). To use its healing properties, hang cinquefoil over your bed when you're ill to get better quickly, or brew an infusion to add into your bathwater to reduce fevers. Take advantage of cinquefoil's mystical associations in the Divination Dream Sachet (page 148).

Comfrey

- **Common Name:** Comfrey
- **Latin Name:** *Symphytum officinale*
- **Folk Name:** Black wort, boneset, slippery root, knit bone
- **Gender:** Feminine
- **Magical Purpose:** Cleansing and purification, divination work, protection, wealth
- **Planetary Ruler:** Saturn
- **Elemental Ruler:** Water

There are several varieties of comfrey, which is part of the borage family and native to Europe and Asia. The root and the leaves are typically used, and it was often cultivated in family gardens because it was so useful in treating wounds and injuries. During the Middle Ages, healers discovered its value in setting broken bones. Comfrey root was boiled into a poultice and applied to the limbs to reduce inflammation, and patients were encouraged to drink a decoction made from the leaves.

Comfrey became a popular item to carry on pilgrimages; not only did it ensure travelers' personal safety, it also helped prevent theft while on the road. It was used in many places as feed for livestock. During Ireland's Great Famine, some families stayed alive by eating boiled comfrey in the absence of other foods.

MAGICAL USES: Comfrey is great for protection—be sure to try the Safe & Secure Smudge Sticks (page 93) and the Protection Oil (page 89). If you're going on a trip, tuck a sachet of comfrey into your suitcases to keep them from being tampered with or stolen. For healing magic, use it in the Healing Comfrey Candle Spell (page 126).

Plant comfrey in decorative pots at your place of business to draw new customers and encourage them to spend money. Comfrey is associated with divination and intuition, so use it in the Spiritual Bath Blend (page 147) and the Moonlight Divination Candle (page 150) spells. In *The Illustrated Herbiary*, author Maia Toll suggests that comfrey is a reminder to our spirit that it's important to do magic in a mindful way, working intuitively and thoughtfully.

Dill

* **Common Name:** Dill
* **Latin Name:** *Anethum graveolens*
* **Folk Name:** Garden dill, dill weed, aneton
* **Gender:** Masculine
* **Magical Purpose:** Love and lust, protection, money
* **Planetary Ruler:** Mercury
* **Elemental Ruler:** Fire

The dill plant, a hardy annual that spreads just about everywhere it's rooted, was recorded in the early writings of Greek philosophers as well as naturalists in the Middle Ages. Although today it's popular in culinary dishes, it has a rich history of medicinal and metaphysical use. During the Renaissance period in Europe, dill was popular in charms against witchcraft and sorcery.

Dill oil can be used as a stimulant and was blended into water prescribed for digestive problems. The seeds of the dill plant are associated with abundance and bounty.

MAGICAL USES: Use dill in protection magic, like the Protection Pouch Sachet Spell (page 89) or the Magical Mayhem Jar Spell (page 98). Plant it in containers near your front door to keep troublemakers away. It is associated with the guardianship of children, so hang dill over a child's bed to keep them safe.

Despite smelling like pickles—or maybe because of it—dill can help attract romance, with the Candle Spell to Bring Love into Your Life (page 107). Associated with wealth and prosperity, dill is great for money workings like the Check Your Wallet spell (page 131) and the Cash Register Charm (page 135). Sprinkle the seeds around your house to draw money and financial fortune into your life.

Eucalyptus ....

* **Common Name:** Eucalyptus
* **Latin Name:** *Eucalyptus globulus*
* **Folk Name:** Blue gum, stringy bark
* **Gender:** Feminine
* **Magical Purpose:** Protection, healing
* **Planetary Ruler:** Moon
* **Elemental Ruler:** Water

The eucalyptus tree has leathery leaves covered with an aromatic oil. It's native to Australia and Tanzania; you've probably seen koalas munching it at the zoo. When European explorers encountered it in the nineteenth century, they learned indigenous people valued it for its medicinal properties and began exporting it to Germany and France. Eucalyptus oil, extracted through distillation, was used as an antiseptic and to treat fevers resulting from tropical diseases like malaria.

Today, eucalyptus oil is found as an ingredient in a number of disinfectants, and the flavoring is popular in cold and cough medicine. Because of its pharmaceutical properties, it's often included in healing spells among folk magic traditions.

MAGICAL USES: Use eucalyptus for protection spells like the Purification Incense Blend (page 94). Keep stalks of it in a pot near your door or on the front step to keep your family safe at home. Put a few fresh leaves in your shoes while you're out and about to stay safe as you travel.

Eucalyptus is known for its healing properties—use it in the Soothing Sachet (page 117), the Healing Oils Laundry Soap (page 121), and the Healing Wreath for the Sickroom (page 124). Hang it over the bed or tuck it under an ill person's pillow to promote overall healing. If you're lucky enough to find some of the small green pods, string them on a blue cord—blue being associated with healing—and wear them as a necklace or bracelet to prevent colds, sore throats, and respiratory ailments.

Feverfew

- Ⓐ **Common Name:** Feverfew
- Ⓐ **Latin Name:** *Tanacetum parthenium*
- Ⓐ **Folk Name:** Febrifuge, featherfoil, bachelor's button, maid's weed
- Ⓐ **Gender:** Masculine
- Ⓐ **Magical Purpose:** Healing, protection
- Ⓐ **Planetary Ruler:** Venus
- Ⓐ **Elemental Ruler:** Water

As you might guess from its name, feverfew has valuable medicinal properties. With a finely furred stem and tiny, daisy-like flowers, feverfew is a low-maintenance plant often found in hedgerows along roadsides. It became a popular perennial among country healers, who valued its curative applications.

Feverfew was known to bring relief from a variety of complaints: A decoction blended with sugar and honey was a standard treatment for coughs, colds, and sore throats, according to English physician Nicholas Culpeper in his *Complete Herbal*. An ointment blended from fresh feverfew could be applied externally to painful and itchy insect bites and stings. Physicians often steeped the flowers to create a tea which, once cooled, was used to allay symptoms of anxiety, depression, and nervousness.

<u>MAGICAL USES:</u> Use feverfew for protection magic—try the Protection Pouch Sachet Spell (page 89). Plant it in hedges along the perimeter walls of your home to keep yourself and your family safe from colds and fevers, as well as to prevent random household accidents.

Feverfew has a long history of healing a variety of ailments; use it to make the Feverfew Charm (page 118) to keep illness away. Hang bundles in a sickroom, or tuck them under the bed of someone who is anxious or feeling blue to promote overall emotional wellness.

Goldenseal ....

- **Common Name:** Goldenseal
- **Latin Name:** *Hydrastis canadensis*
- **Folk Name:** Eye balm, Indian paint, turmeric root, jaundice root, wild curcuma, orange root
- **Gender:** Masculine
- **Magical Purpose:** Money, healing
- **Planetary Ruler:** Sun
- **Elemental Ruler:** Fire

Indigenous to North America, goldenseal is part of the buttercup family and is highly prized by herbalists for its medicinal properties, according to botanist Judith Sumner, author of *American Household Botany*. It's been used among the Cherokee in treatment of cancerous diseases and digestive disorders, in addition to serving as a diuretic and an effective eyewash. It was also processed into a yellow dye for clothing and weaponry.

In the late twentieth century, goldenseal was placed on the list of plant species threatened with endangerment, thanks to overharvesting. In many parts of the United States and Canada, collecting goldenseal on public lands is prohibited, or may require a permit. If you'd like to use goldenseal in your magic, be sure you're purchasing it from someone who has gathered it ethically. An even better alternative is to cultivate your own for magical use; it's a bit labor-intensive, but it's rewarding to know you're preserving an heirloom species.

MAGICAL USES: Use goldenseal in healing magic, like the Get Better Bath Spell (page 123). Create a sachet or pillow out of flannel, sew goldenseal root into it along with other healing herbs, and tuck it into the mattress of someone suffering from long-term illness or chronic pain.

When it comes to money magic, goldenseal is a handy herb to have in your witchy tool kit—use it in the Bountiful Blessings Incense (page 136) and the Get the Jump on the Job Salve (page 139). Anoint a green or gold candle with a base oil and roll it in powdered goldenseal to attract wealth. Goldenseal is a magical booster herb; add it to any other spell to give that working some extra power. Keep a sprinkling of dried goldenseal on your altar to help you connect with the Divine.

High John the Conqueror ....

- ❀ **Common Name:** High John the Conqueror
- ❀ **Latin Name:** *Ipomoea jalapa*
- ❀ **Folk Name:** John the Conqueror root
- ❀ **Gender:** Masculine
- ❀ **Magical Purpose:** Success and power, love, lust and sexual potency, money
- ❀ **Planetary Ruler:** Mars
- ❀ **Elemental Ruler:** Fire

Named for an African folk hero, High John the Conqueror is extremely popular in folk magic systems such as Hoodoo and other African traditional practices. Related to the sweet potato and the morning glory, High John has a warm, earthy smell and is used regularly in amulet bags.

High John is best known for its use in magic related to sexual potency and the drawing of money, particularly in gambling and games of chance. Because the root is a tuber that has some pretty potent laxative properties, it's **important not to use High John internally**.

MAGICAL USES: High John can protect you from curses or hexes, particularly those causing sexual dysfunction, so carry a piece of the root in your pocket or tuck it under your mattress to protect yourself. It's also a powerful ingredient in love magic, so use it in your Pocket Love Charm (page 105). Hang a High John root in a bright red bag over your bed to revitalize your sex life.

Associated with wealth and power, High John can be used for talismans related to abundance—try the Prosperity Pocket Charm (page 133) and the Cash Register Charm (page 135). If you own a business, tie a High John root in a gold cloth and hang it near the door; when customers come in, they'll be inclined to spend more money. Carry a piece in a green cloth bag to draw wealth. Mix pieces of High John into water and use it as a wash for your floors, doors, and windows to take back decision-making power in your home.

Hyssop

- **Common Name:** Hyssop
- **Latin Name:** *Hyssopus officinalis*
- **Folk Name:** Isopo, yssop, azob or ezov (Biblical)
- **Gender:** Masculine
- **Magical Purpose:** Purification, protection, healing
- **Planetary Ruler:** Jupiter
- **Elemental Ruler:** Fire

The documented use of hyssop in purification and religious ceremonies is older than classical times. Part of the mint family, and native to the Middle East and southern Europe, hyssop was often cultivated for its fragrant pink flowers, which were brewed into an infusion used as an

antiseptic and to treat coughs. Although it's sometimes found in culinary applications in broths and salads, the primary use of hyssop has
been medicinal.

Although the hyssop cultivated in Europe isn't the same hyssop
mentioned in the Bible (which is referred to alternately as *azob* or *ezov*),
the plant has been used in purification, both physical and spiritual. In
particular, it became a valuable addition to the practice of respiratory
cleansing and was often strewn along dirt floors in England and colonial
America. Hyssop was also known for its ability to keep insects away.
**Avoid using hyssop during pregnancy, including handling the
essential oil.**

MAGICAL USES: For protection, use hyssop in the Herbal Braid (page 91),
Home Purification Wash for Floors & Doors (page 93), and Protection
Oil (page 89). Hang bundles of hyssop in your windows to keep evil and
negativity from entering, or place some of the dried leaves on a charcoal
disc and burn them as incense, waving the smoke around to purify your
house. It smells strong, but it will drive away anything unpleasant that
has come to visit. Brew an infusion, and sprinkle it around the perimeter
of your property to purify the area and keep it safe from ill intentions.

For wellness magic, use hyssop in the Healing Water Hand Wash
(page 120) and Happy Healthy Whole Poppet (page 123) spells. Hang it
above your bed for overall health.

Lavender ....

- **Common Name:** Lavender
- **Latin Name:** *Lavandula angustifolia*
- **Folk Name:** Spike, elf leaf, nard
- **Gender:** Masculine
- **Magical Purpose:** Cleansing and purification, calming dreams, relaxation, love
- **Planetary Ruler:** Mercury
- **Elemental Ruler:** Air

Common lavender, formerly classified as *Lavandula officinalis*, is a shrubby plant with long stems and fragrant purple flowers. Lavender is prized for both its aromatic blossoms and its essential oil, which is incorporated into aromatherapy, perfume making, and other applications. There are numerous varieties, and you can use any of them in magic; the most common strains are English and French lavender.

The Greeks called lavender *nard*, after the ancient city of Naarda. Ancient Romans used it to scent their clothing and bath water; its name comes from the Latin *lavare*, which means "to wash." Thanks to its fragrance, lavender water gained popularity throughout Europe, and women used it to attract lovers. For centuries, lavender oil dabbed behind the ears was a custom among prostitutes seeking clients. In *Garden Witchery,* author Ellen Dugan reminds us that lavender has long been a popular ingredient in potpourri and cosmetics.

MAGICAL USES: Lavender is associated with protection magic, so hang a bundle in your home. Use it in the Herbal Braid (page 91), the Protective Wreath to Guard Your Door (page 92), and the Safe & Secure Smudge Sticks (page 93). Place a few fresh stalks under your pillow to aid in dreaming and calm sleep or burn the dried flowers on a charcoal disc to alleviate insomnia. Carry a lavender sachet to inhale whenever you feel stressed, and let its soft fragrance soothe your nerves.

Lavender's romantic smell makes it perfect for love magic. Keep a vase of freshly cut lavender stalks in your bedroom to bring passion into your life. Blend some Lavender Love Incense (page 103), a Self-Love Bath Bomb Bag (page 109), or an Herbal Beauty Glamour Spell (page 110). Healing magic never smelled so good—try the Healing Oils Laundry Soap (page 121), the Stress-Relief Smudge Sticks (page 121), and the Soothing Lavender Pillow (page 122).

Mandrake

- **Common Name:** Mandrake
- **Latin Name:** *Mandragora officinarum*
- **Folk Name:** Brain thief, gallows herb, witches' mannikin, wild lemon, sorcerer's root, Satan's apple
- **Gender:** Masculine
- **Magical Purpose:** Lust and fertility, money, protection
- **Planetary Ruler:** Mercury
- **Elemental Ruler:** Fire

The mandrake root has a distinctive appearance—it's large, brown, and shaped almost like a human body. The ancients used it for several purposes: By boiling it in milk and adding it to a poultice, mandrake was a treatment for suppurative ulcers. Some early physicians prescribed it to alleviate pain or convulsions. Taken internally in large doses, however, it was said to cause madness.

Historically, mandrake roots, leaves, and bark have all been used both medicinally and magically. Anglo-Saxon practitioners used it against demonic possession, and a number of folk tales about mandrake have survived through the ages. There are accounts of witches during England's Tudor period using roots as poppets, in which they stood in for people who were the targets of malevolent magic. Mandrake allegedly flourished beneath gallows poles, leading to several related folkloric names.

MAGICAL USES: Mandrake is highly useful in protection magic, especially against enchantment or possession. It's hard to come by, and a bit expensive, but if you're fortunate enough to find a whole mandrake root, it's traditional to keep it prominently displayed in your home to keep evil and negativity away. If you want to guard against theft, try out the Keep Your Car Covered Protection Charm (page 95).

Did you know mandrake can be used in love magic? Make a Self-Love Bath Bomb Bag (page 109) or the Fertility Amulet (page 111). Since mandrake is also associated with wealth, place bits of the dried leaves in your wallet to double your money. To boost your bank account, use the Mandrake Money Manifestation spell (page 133).

Mistletoe

- **Common Name:** Mistletoe
- **Latin Name:** *Viscum album*
- **Folk Name:** Witches' broom, golden bough, all heal, *herbe de la croix*, holy wood
- **Gender:** Masculine
- **Magical Purpose:** Healing, protection, exorcism
- **Planetary Ruler:** Sun
- **Elemental Ruler:** Air

Mistletoe is a staple of winter with its bright green leaves, tiny yellowish-white flowers, and small berries.

The Druids performed rituals in which they harvested mistletoe from oak trees and then fed it to livestock to ensure abundance in the coming year. The Romans performed fertility rites under boughs of mistletoe in honor of the agricultural god Saturn during his annual festival—perhaps this is one of the origins of our tradition of kissing beneath it! Although associated with conception and fertility, **mistletoe is poisonous, and the berries and leaves can be fatal to children and pregnant or nursing women**.

MAGICAL USES: Use mistletoe for protection work with the Purification Incense Blend (page 94). Hang a sprig over your door to welcome peace and keep negative energy away. During the winter holidays, weave boughs of it into your decorations and protect your family from those who might wish you malice. For love magic, place dried mistletoe in a pillow or sachet to tuck under your pillow to attract romance, or make a poppet representing your ideal lover wearing a crown of mistletoe.

In healing magic, mistletoe is a great addition to the Healing Incense Blend (page 117). Carry a bit of dried mistletoe wood in your pocket or on a cord around your neck to keep illness away. Dress a blue candle with powdered mistletoe leaves to burn for overall wellness. Mistletoe has long been associated with divination work—incorporate it into your Spiritual Bath Blend (page 147) and the Herbal Pendulum Magic spell (page 153).

Mugwort......................................

- ⊛ **Common Name:** Mugwort
- ⊛ **Latin Name:** *Artemisia vulgaris*
- ⊛ **Folk Name:** Artemis plant, felon's herb, old man, Uncle Henry, sailor's tobacco, Saint John's cingulum
- ⊛ **Gender:** Feminine
- ⊛ **Magical Purpose:** Divination and spirit work, intuition, psychic abilities, protection
- ⊛ **Planetary Ruler:** Venus
- ⊛ **Elemental Ruler:** Earth

Mugwort refers to a number of different plants in various parts of the world. Common mugwort, *artemisia vulgaris*, can be grown in just about any soil conditions. It has fairly tall stalks, sometimes reaching three feet or higher, with dark green leaves and pinkish or yellow flowers. Roman soldiers were encouraged to use mugwort salve on their feet to prevent fatigue during long marches. During the Middle Ages, it was called *cingulum Sancti Johannis*, because St. John the Baptist wore a belt of mugwort as he traveled to protect him from evil spirits.

North America's indigenous people used mugwort tea to treat fever and other ailments. Plants could be brewed into an infusion to cure stomach disorders or added to bathwater to help patients feel invigorated. **Avoid using mugwort during pregnancy, particularly the essential oil.**

MAGICAL USES: Carry mugwort in your shoes or pockets for both protection and a feeling of rejuvenation. Hang bundles of it over your door to prevent evil spirits or harmful magic from entering. Mugwort is beneficial for overall wellness—use it in the Magical Mugwort Healing Dreams spell (page 119) or the Healing Wreath for the Sickroom (page 124).

Mugwort has powerful divinatory applications, so stuff leaves into a sachet or pillow for astral projection, dream magic, and prophecy. Use it for some Mugwort Moon Magic (page 145), the Inspirational Intuition Incense Blend (page 149), or the Open Your Third Eye spell (page 151). Brew an infusion of mugwort to cleanse your divination tools, such as crystals, pendulums, or scrying mirrors.

Mullein ....

- **Common Name:** Mullein
- **Latin Name:** *Verbascum thapsus*
- **Folk Name:** Blanket leaf, candlewick, hag's taper, feltwort, graveyard dust, shepherd's club, velvetback
- **Gender:** Feminine
- **Magical Purpose:** Divination, courage, strength, protection
- **Planetary Ruler:** Saturn
- **Elemental Ruler:** Fire

There are several members of the mullein family, and all can be used in magic. This plant's downy leaves and stem were used for lamp wicks before cotton was introduced; there's a legend that witches used it to provide light in secret rituals. In England, farmers fed their livestock mullein to prevent respiratory ailments, and it was used for protection from evil spirits and baneful magic.

During the Middle Ages mullein was used in decoctions for treating pleurisy and consumption, and Nicholas Culpeper recommended poultices made from the leaves be applied to piles (hemorrhoids) and frostbitten skin. The dried roots were rubbed on warts to eliminate them, and in some traditions of folk magic, mullein was included in love divination. Like patchouli, dried and powdered mullein has a dusty quality, and it's sometimes incorporated into spells calling for graveyard dust.

MAGICAL USES: Mix up mullein for protective magic and make some Purification Incense Blend (page 94). Place leaves in your shoe if you go hiking to keep yourself safe on the trail. Stuff a sachet with mullein and place it in your pillow to keep nightmares away. Hang it over your doors and windows to keep negativity from entering your home.

Mullein is useful in love magic; sprinkle the dried and powdered leaves in the footsteps of the person you're attracted to, and they'll find you appealing as well. Take advantage of its prophetic properties and make a Divination Dream Sachet (page 148) or do the Self-Awareness Spell (page 151).

Nettle ....

- **Common Name:** Nettle
- **Latin Name:** *Urtica dioica*
- **Folk Name:** Stinging nettle
- **Gender:** Masculine
- **Magical Purpose:** Protection, exorcism, healing
- **Planetary Ruler:** Mars
- **Elemental Ruler:** Fire

The stinging nettle plant blooms in the wild all summer in many places, including Europe and Asia. The magical and medicinal properties of nettle are well-known; Roman soldiers discovered that nettles applied to the skin helped alleviate aches and pains caused by Britain's damp climate.

Many healers claimed they could cure fever simply by pulling up a nettle by its root and calling out the name of the patient as they did so. In some areas, it was believed that if you gathered nettle before sunrise, it protected your cattle from evil spirits and vengeful witches.

<u>MAGICAL USES:</u> If you're careful, you can use nettle in protection magic; watch out for the poky hairs that give this stinging herb its name. Work up the Protection Pouch Sachet Spell (page 89) and the Spell to Stop a Gossip (page 98). Plant nettle in your yard to keep ghosts and malevolent spirits away. If you think someone has hexed you, make a poppet to represent them, stuff it with stinging nettle, and throw it into a moving body of water to remove the curse.

It's hard to believe something so irritating and itchy could be used in a love spell, but the Heartbreak Healer (page 109) is a great way to bounce back from a bad romance, and dried nettle burned as an incense can invigorate passion and lust. Use nettle in healing spells, like the Anxiety Jar (page 125) or the Spell for Post-Trauma Healing (page 126), or place a vase of nettle stalks in a sickroom to alleviate illness. Nettle is also associated with divination—use it for the Self-Awareness Spell (page 151).

Patchouli ....

- **Common Name:** Patchouli
- **Latin Name:** *Pogostemon cablin*
- **Folk Name:** Pucha pot, pucha-pat, graveyard dust
- **Gender:** Feminine
- **Magical Purpose:** Love and lust, fertility, money
- **Planetary Ruler:** Saturn
- **Elemental Ruler:** Earth

Patchouli originates in India, but its distinct, earthy smell is known the world over and has long been associated with lust and fertility. Used in sachets packed around exported cloths, patchouli caught the attention of Europeans in the nineteenth century. French perfume makers soon realized that the exotic aroma could help them grow their fortunes.

As a member of the mint family, the dried leaves and essential oils are the most popular parts of the patchouli plant, but some practitioners also use the stems and the small, purplish-white flowers. The mysterious scent is found in incense blends and potpourri. In some folk magic traditions, powdered patchouli is referred to as graveyard dust.

MAGICAL USES: Patchouli is delightfully fragrant, so a little goes a long way. It's a sexy, sensual smell, which makes it perfect for love magic like the Love Poppets (page 105), the Patchouli Passion spell (page 108), and the Fertility Amulet (page 111). To make someone more attracted to you, wear diluted patchouli oil—the scent is well-known as an aphrodisiac. If you don't wish to wear the oil on your skin, use the leaves instead; place them in a sachet and carry it in your pocket or wear it around your neck to attract your romantic interests.

For money magic, try the Patchouli Payoff Bath spell (page 137) and Wealth Wash for Your Home (page 138). Use patchouli oil to inscribe a dollar sign on a piece of paper; fold this up and keep it in your wallet to draw money your way. Dress a green candle with a base oil, roll it in dried and powdered patchouli leaves, and burn it during the waxing moon to attract abundance.

Pennyroyal

- **Common Name:** Pennyroyal
- **Latin Name:** *Mentha pulegium*
- **Folk Name:** Run-by-the-ground, lurk-in-the-ditch, organ broth, tick weed, pudding grass
- **Gender:** Masculine
- **Magical Purpose:** Protection and strength, peace
- **Planetary Ruler:** Mars
- **Elemental Ruler:** Fire

Known for its ability to drive away fleas and ticks, pennyroyal often appears along roadsides at random. It grows all over Europe and the Americas and was popular as a tea plant used to treat colds, nervous disorders, and other ailments. Greek physicians recommended their patients hang it in the sickroom, and even placed leaves into stagnant water to remove toxins.

In the Americas, pennyroyal was traditionally used by indigenous women to promote menstrual flow and as a method of contraception. According to Maud Grieve in *A Modern Herbal*, pennyroyal is an abortifacient and stimulates uterine contraction; **avoid using pennyroyal essential oil during pregnancy**.

MAGICAL USES: Pennyroyal has powerful protective properties—include it in the Protective Wreath to Guard Your Door (page 92). If you're arguing with someone, rub the leaves between your fingertips; when you come to terms of accord, shake the person's hand and pennyroyal will promote ongoing peace. Keep a bowl of fresh pennyroyal in your home—ideally, in a common area that all family members use—to keep people from quarrelling. Carry a pennyroyal sachet in your pocket to ward off the evil eye or hang it around your home to prevent harmful magic.

Pennyroyal's healing properties are known around the world, so use it in wellness magic. Keep some of the leaves in your shoes to feel fresh and energized, especially if you've got a busy day planned. Use the leaves to make an infusion and, once it cools, wash your hands and feet to keep sickness away. Tie a bag of pennyroyal to your bedpost to help sharpen your wits and increase mental and spiritual clarity.

Peppermint ....

- **Common Name:** Peppermint
- **Latin Name:** *Mentha piperita*
- **Folk Name:** Brandy mint, lammint
- **Gender:** Masculine
- **Magical Purpose:** Cleansing and purification, protection, sleep and dreams, healing, love
- **Planetary Ruler:** Mercury
- **Elemental Ruler:** Fire

There are dozens of members of the fragrant mint family, and they're often associated with healing and purification. If you decide to grow your own peppermint, be sure to plant it in a container; it's highly invasive and will spread into your entire yard if you don't keep it in check. The Greeks and Romans of classical times wore crowns of peppermint during festivals and used it to flavor their rich wines and sauces.

There is evidence that the Egyptians deliberately cultivated peppermint, and it also appears in the Icelandic pharmacopoeias of the medieval period. Peppermint oil, which is harvested from different strains, is an anti-spasmodic, and holistic healers often use it to treat problems with the digestive system. Peppermint oil can also be used to fight off coughs, colds, and fevers. Be careful to dilute peppermint oil before using it topically; undiluted, the oil will cause irritation.

MAGICAL USES: Nearly everyone loves the smell of peppermint, which makes it a deliciously subtle ingredient in protection magic like the Protection Pocket Charm (page 90). Keep sprigs of fresh peppermint around your home, both to freshen the air and to keep evil energy away. Rub the leaves on your magical tools to cleanse them, particularly if they've been handled by people who would wish you harm.

Feeling like you need a bit of romance in your life? Incorporate peppermint into a pair of Love Poppets (page 105). Serve a glass of mint tea to someone you care about and watch your love life flourish. Burn the dried leaves on a charcoal disc as incense when you're about to get intimate with a partner; the smoke can be a powerful aphrodisiac. Don't disregard peppermint's healing powers—use it in a Soothing Sachet (page 117) or the Stress-Relief Smudge Sticks (page 121).

Rosemary ....

- **Common Name:** Rosemary
- **Latin Name:** *Rosmarinus officinalis*
- **Folk Name:** Compass weed, dew of the sea, polar plant, elf leaf
- **Gender:** Masculine
- **Magical Purpose:** Remembrance, protection, purification, healing, love, mental acuity, inspiration
- **Planetary Ruler:** Sun
- **Elemental Ruler:** Fire

Rosemary is a highly aromatic perennial—you've probably got some in your kitchen spice rack for use in cooking. It thrives in warmer climates but is surprisingly hardy and will survive in cooler areas as well. Rosemary plants can live for decades if well cared for.

The fragrant leaves are familiar to chefs, but rosemary also has a long magical and medicinal history. Thanks to its association with memory in the ancient world, going back as early as 5000 BCE, it's become the preferred emblem of fidelity between lovers. Brides in the medieval period entwined it in the wreaths they wore. **Avoid using rosemary essential oil during pregnancy.**

MAGICAL USES: Fresh or dried rosemary can be used in a number of magical ways. Place it beneath your pillow to conjure dreams of lost family members and for protection from harm. Hang fresh sprigs on your door to keep out negative energy, or burn dried leaves as incense prior to magical workings to keep yourself safe. Use it in the Protection Pocket Charm (page 90), the Safe & Secure Smudge Sticks (page 93), and the Peaceful Protection Potted Plant (page 96).

For love magic, try the Rosemary Remembrance for Long-Lost Love spell (page 112). Make an infusion of rosemary steeped in warm water to wash your hands before doing healing magic, or as a revitalizing facial wash when you're feeling off-kilter. To boost your intuitive abilities, use rosemary in the Divination Dream Sachet (page 148) and the Clarity Smudge Sticks (page 152). Keep it in your magical workspace if you're calling ancestral guides.

Rue

- **Common Name:** Rue
- **Latin Name:** *Ruta graveolens*
- **Folk Name:** Herb of grace, mother of herbs, ruta, herbygrass, herb of repentance
- **Gender:** Masculine
- **Magical Purpose:** Protection and exorcism, healing, love
- **Planetary Ruler:** Mars
- **Elemental Ruler:** Fire

An ornamental plant with a pungent smell, rue is found in gardens around the world. In ancient Rome, physicians combined rue with other plants to cure snakebite and to stimulate menstruation. It made its way into Europe as an addition to culinary creations, and Italian painters believed it helped improve vision.

During celebrations of High Mass, holy water was sprinkled using brushes of rue leaves, earning it the nickname *herb of repentance*. Many people used it for bedding during the Middle Ages, as its harsh aroma may have kept fleas and other insects at bay. Rue was known to repel the evil eye. **Avoid using rue if you are pregnant or nursing.**

MAGICAL USES: Rue has a strong, earthy smell that not everyone finds appealing, but it works beautifully for protection spells. Weave it into your Safe & Secure Smudge Sticks (page 93) and blend it into the Home Purification Wash for Floors & Doors (page 93). Hang rue around your property to keep malevolent magic out and trespassers away, both the human and four-legged varieties. Scatter leaves on your floors to return negative spells back to the sender.

For romance, use rue in the Candle Spell to Bring Love into Your Life (page 107). Carry a sachet of rue to sniff when you need to make big decisions about relationships. Rue has valuable healing properties as well—use it in the Spell to Soothe a Savage Cycle (page 119) if you're struggling with an uncomfortable period, and add it into the Get Better Bath Spell (page 123) for overall wellness.

Sage

- **Common Name:** Sage
- **Latin Name:** *Salvia officinalis*
- **Folk Name:** Sawge, garden sage, salvia savatrix
- **Gender:** Masculine
- **Magical Purpose:** Cleansing and purification, intuition and wisdom, psychic gifts
- **Planetary Ruler:** Jupiter
- **Elemental Ruler:** Air

There are numerous types of sage, and nearly all have been used in spiritual practice. Common sage is an acceptable substitute for other varieties, particularly those that are endangered or at risk of overcultivation. Sage's natural habitat is around the Mediterranean, but it will grow just about anywhere; it's a hardy perennial popular in ornamental and kitchen gardens.

During the Middle Ages, European physicians used sage as a curative for palsy, fever, and anxious nerves, and they believed eating some daily would help you live a long and healthy life. If sage was planted in front of your business, the condition of your plants reflected that of your success; flourishing leaves and flowers meant you were doing well, but if your sage withered, so would your trade. In Asia, sage is sometimes used in tea to improve memory and relieve the symptoms of arthritis. **Avoid using sage essential oil during pregnancy.**

<u>MAGICAL USES:</u> Burn dried sage on a charcoal disc to drive spirits out of your home—but be careful not to evict good spirits along with the bad. Plant sage seedlings around your yard to keep troublemakers away. Rub a fresh leaf between your hands before engaging in conflict as you make a wish for your intended outcome.

Keep fresh sage on hand for healing magic. Place a few sprigs under your pillow if you're anxious or have trouble sleeping. If you're restless because of grief or depression, sage can help alleviate your symptoms. Sage has been used in spiritual ceremonies around the world for ages and can help you connect to your divinatory work—make a Psychic Amulet (page 145), the Moonlight Divination Candle (page 150), and the Clarity Smudge Sticks (page 152).

Sandalwood ....

- **Common Name:** Sandalwood
- **Latin Name:** *Santalum album*
- **Folk Name:** Sanders-wood, white saunders, santal
- **Gender:** Feminine
- **Magical Purpose:** Cleansing and purification, protection, exorcism
- **Planetary Ruler:** Moon
- **Elemental Ruler:** Water

Although not truly an herb, sandalwood is used in a variety of religious rituals, aromatherapy, and medicine around the world. Technically, sandalwood is an entire class of wood, found in the trees of the flowering Santalum family and packed with essential oils. Because Indian sandalwood is at risk from overharvesting, most sandalwood sold in the United States and Europe comes from the non-endangered Australian variety. Be sure you're only using sandalwood that is ethically sourced.

In Ayurvedic medicine, sandalwood oil has been used to treat ailments from bronchitis to sexually transmitted infections. Because the wood is sacred, it was often used in the construction of Indian temples, religious statues, and spiritual tools, which could stay fragrant for decades. It's said that burning sandalwood as incense will stimulate the crown chakra, which brings us closer to the Divine and helps with achieving spiritual clarity.

MAGICAL USES: Sandalwood is associated with cleansing, so burn it as incense prior to rituals, or to purify your home or workspace. Place pieces of the wood around your home for protection from negative energy or evil spirits. If you think you've been cursed or hexed, mark a piece of sandalwood with the name of the person who is causing you trouble and burn it outside your home, then take the ashes far away and bury them or scatter them into the wind.

Sandalwood has a rich, musky aroma and can help with workings related to divination and developing your psychic abilities. Use it in the Spiritual Bath Blend (page 147), the Sandalwood Clairvoyance Spell (page 154), and the Open Your Third Eye spell (page 151). Make a necklace of sandalwood beads or drill a hole in a chunk of the wood and wear it on a cord to develop additional spiritual awareness.

Thistle ....

- **Common Name:** Common thistle
- **Latin Name:** *Cirsium vulgare*
- **Folk Name:** Spear thistle, bull thistle, Scotch thistle
- **Gender:** Masculine
- **Magical Purpose:** Healing and strength, hex-breaking
- **Planetary Ruler:** Mars
- **Elemental Ruler:** Fire

There are numerous varieties of thistle, but the common thistle is often found on land left untended—you'll see it growing in ditches, along roadsides, or on properties that have been abandoned and left to the elements. In fact, thistles tend to be invasive, taking over and pushing other plants out of the way. But don't let the thistle fool you—it provides a valuable service, providing nectar for pollinators from its bright purple flowers.

The thistle is a multi-purpose plant, every part of it valuable. In *A Modern Herbal*, Maud Grieve says that the juice can be applied to skin lesions and ulcers, the leaves are often included in salads, the roots can be mashed into a poultice to treat toothache, and the steamed flowers can alleviate nervous conditions and rheumatic aches and pains.

MAGICAL USES: Thistles are sharp and poky, making them perfect for protection magic. Plant a border around your property to keep thieves and troublemakers out. Hang dried stalks above your door to repel negative energy. If you've got someone causing problems, do the Magical Mayhem Jar Spell (page 98). Use thistles to break a curse: Create a poppet to represent yourself, light dried thistles on fire, and place the poppet above the flames so the curse is carried away on the smoke.

Take some dried thistle, grind it into powder, and sprinkle it into your shoes—this brings about physical strength and stamina and can improve your love life. Use thistle for healing magic, like the Anxiety Jar (page 125). Carry a thistle flower as a charm for overall wellness and rejuvenation when you're run down and exhausted. For divination work, boil fresh thistle flowers in a pot over an open fire; watch the steam for visions and images.

Thyme

- ❂ **Common Name:** Thyme
- ❂ **Latin Name:** *Thymus vulgaris*
- ❂ **Folk Name:** Garden thyme, common thyme
- ❂ **Gender:** Feminine
- ❂ **Magical Purpose:** Courage, sleep and dreams, healing, psychic abilities
- ❂ **Planetary Ruler:** Venus
- ❂ **Elemental Ruler:** Water

Although it originally grew wild in the mountains of Spain, thyme has evolved so that what we use now is a deliberately cultivated variety that grows in just about any temperate climate. The Greeks named early versions of thyme with a word that meant *to fumigate*, and they burned it as a sweet-smelling incense in spiritual ceremonies. Physicians of the classical period used thyme for its antiseptic properties; Dioscorides recommended its use to cure inflammations of the liver.

During the Middle Ages, people used thyme for its powers of invigoration and ability to inspire courage. Practitioners in this period knew that if they pounded the leaves to release thyme's essential oils, they could mix it into a syrup to treat whooping cough and sore throats, or brew it into a tea to reduce colic or help break a fever. **Avoid using thyme essential oil during pregnancy.**

MAGICAL USES: Burn dried thyme leaves on a charcoal disc as an incense to purify your space; pass your magical tools through the rising smoke to metaphysically cleanse them. Stuff it into sachets or pillows and tuck them under your mattress to bring about peaceful sleep. If you're facing a challenge, brew the leaves into an infusion and, once it cools, dab a bit on your pulse points to help you conquer your fears and give you courage under pressure.

Blend sprigs of thyme with lavender and hang them over the bed in a sickroom to bring about recovery. During a major housecleaning, add thyme to warm water and use it to wash floors and windows, promoting overall health in your home. Thyme can also be incorporated into workings related to wisdom and guidance—try the Thyme Teller Guidance Charm (page 149) and the Awakening Oil (page 154) during your divination rituals.

Tobacco Leaf.............................

- **Common Name:** Tobacco
- **Latin Name:** *Nicotiana tabacum*
- **Folk Name:** Tobacky, tabacca
- **Gender:** Masculine
- **Magical Purpose:** Cleansing and purification, divination, spirit communication
- **Planetary Ruler:** Mars
- **Elemental Ruler:** Fire

Tobacco leaves appear in spiritual ceremonies worldwide as both an offering and a magical component. Although there are different varieties, commercially grown tobacco is often seen as an acceptable magical substitute for the other strains, including wild tobacco (*nicotiana rustica*). Cultivated in the Americas from about one thousand years ago, the large, flat leaves are typically hung up to dry and then crushed for use. Indigenous peoples carried tobacco blends to trade as social and ceremonial offerings, according to author Harold Roth in *The Witching Herbs*.

Once Europeans figured out tobacco could be smoked, it became a popular commodity, and English and Spanish physicians soon figured out they could promote it for its alleged health benefits. Many claimed it could prevent disease and open the passages of the body to let toxins escape. However, **tobacco is highly poisonous**: Don't chew or eat the leaves, or drink a tea made from them. Wear gloves if you're handling raw leaves while they're fresh or green, because nicotine can be absorbed through the skin.

MAGICAL USES: Burn tobacco on a charcoal disc to purify a sacred space or to drive malevolent spirits away. For those who suffer from bad dreams, place a sachet of dried tobacco under the pillow to alleviate nightmares.

Use tobacco for divinatory work with the Herbal Scrying spell (page 147) and the Moonlight Divination Candle (page 150). To send a message to the spirit world, write your thoughts on an uncrushed dried leaf and burn it; your message will travel away on the smoke. If you'd prefer not to burn it for health reasons, simply scatter the dried leaves around your work area.

Valerian ....

- ✿ **Common Name:** Valerian
- ✿ **Latin Name:** *Valeriana officinalis*
- ✿ **Folk Name:** All heal, amantilla, garden heliotrope, set well, setwall, vandal root
- ✿ **Gender:** Feminine
- ✿ **Magical Purpose:** Love, sleep and dreams, purification, protection
- ✿ **Planetary Ruler:** Venus
- ✿ **Elemental Ruler:** Water

Valerian has a pungent, earthy aroma that makes it distinctive; some people say it smells like dirty gym socks or cat urine. The root is the most commonly used part of the plant in both medicine and magic. Despite the smell of the root, the pink and white flowers have a soft, pleasant fragrance, making it a popular ornamental plant in butterfly gardens.

Physicians in the ancient world used valerian to treat many maladies, from insomnia and anxiety to croup and epilepsy. Cats find it appealing, perhaps because of its strong smell, so your feline friends may react to it as they do catnip.

MAGICAL USES: Use valerian in protection magic and include it in the Magical Mayhem Jar Spell (page 98). Hang a few sprigs around the outside of your house to protect from a lightning strike. The smell of valerian is a sharp one, but it's still used in a lot of traditional love magic—try the Va-va-va-voom Valerian Oil (page 106) to add spice to your love life. Sprinkle it in your shoes when you're with the person you're attracted to, and they'll be compelled to follow your lead.

If you're suffering from the aftershocks of trauma, use it in the Spell for Post-Trauma Healing (page 126). Include valerian in your divination workings, like the Herbal Scrying spell (page 147). Make a pillow or sachet to tuck under your pillow if you have problems sleeping, and it will prevent unpleasant dreams. If there's hostility in the air, hanging valerian in your home will help promote peace and understanding.

Vervain ....

* **Common Name:** Vervain
* **Latin Name:** *Verbena officinalis*
* **Folk Name:** Herb of grace, holy herb, Herb-of-the-cross, pigeon's grass, holy wort, Enchanter's herb
* **Gender:** Feminine
* **Magical Purpose:** Love, empowerment, prosperity
* **Planetary Ruler:** Venus
* **Elemental Ruler:** Water, Earth

For many ancient cultures, vervain was a sacred plant used in healing magic. Early Egyptians claimed it sprung from the tears of Isis mourning her lost husband, Osiris. During the Middle Ages, it became popular in folk magic and appeared in grimoires as an ingredient in witches' potions. Harold Roth says in *The Witching Herbs* that it may have been included in the legendary flying ointment used by witches in the medieval period.

Over time, vervain became known as an all-purpose medicinal herb. It was used to treat everything from throat inflammation and tooth infections to jaundice and abdominal complaints, and it can protect you from snake bites. In herbal medicine, it's the light purple flowers of the vervain plant that are used the most; they're often brewed into a bitter tea or added to a poultice. Because vervain is a uterine stimulant, **be cautious using vervain if you're pregnant**.

MAGICAL USES: Plant vervain around your home to keep negative energy and harm out of your life. Steep some fresh cuttings in an infusion and use the water to consecrate your altar and magical tools. Place sprigs in a sachet beneath a new baby's crib mattress to protect the child and to ensure a life of abundance. Brew up a batch of Vervain Water (page 97) for overall protection magic.

Vervain can be used in workings related to love—not just to draw it into your life, but also to heal from heartbreak. Blend the dried leaves with other love herbs and burn it on a charcoal disc to attract romance or to help you recover from an unexpected breakup. Try the Self-Love Bath Bomb Bag spell (page 109). Vervain can give your bank account a boost. Put fresh leaves in a bottle or bag to wear as a talisman or tuck them into your wallet to multiply your money. Blend vervain into the Bountiful Blessings Incense (page 136), or use it in the Piggy Bank Money Magic spell (page 140).

Vetivert..

- **Common Name:** Vetivert
- **Latin Name:** *Vetiveria zizanioides*
- **Folk Name:** Vetiver, khus, cuscus, iwarancuse
- **Gender:** Feminine
- **Magical Purpose:** Hex-breaking, protection from theft, love and lust
- **Planetary Ruler:** Venus
- **Elemental Ruler:** Earth

Native to India, vetivert (or vetiver) grows best in tropical areas and can even be found in the southern part of the United States. In addition to being used for animal feed and to prevent erosion in fields, vetivert oil is extracted and included in a number of cosmetic applications.

People in parts of West Africa knew that vetivert had sterilizing properties and sometimes added the chopped-up roots to jugs of water to prevent bacteria forming. The fragrant oil can also be used as an anti-fungal and to repel insects like termites. It's often found in perfumes and aromatherapy because of its soft, romantic smell.

MAGICAL USES: Use vetivert root in protection workings against harmful magic with the Purification Incense Blend (page 94) and the Protection Oil (page 89). If you're concerned about robbery, plant vetivert in pots around your house, hang the roots up near your doors and windows, or burn on a charcoal disc to keep thieves away. Use the essential oil or the smoke from vetivert incense to cleanse and purify crystals and divination tools.

To feel lovable and appealing, add vetivert to the Self-Love Bath Bomb Bag (page 109). Anoint your pulse points with a bit of the oil diluted into a base; it's an especially popular herb to use in same-sex love magic. Include vetivert in magic for emotional wellness, particularly if you're struggling to heal from grief or depression, by stuffing it into a pillow or sachet and carrying it with you. If you run a business, tuck a bit of vetivert under your cash register to help boost your sales.

Witch Hazel ....

- ❋ **Common Name:** Witch hazel
- ❋ **Latin Name:** *Hamamelis virginiana*
- ❋ **Folk Name:** Spotted alder, snapping hazelnut, winter bloom
- ❋ **Gender:** Masculine
- ❋ **Magical Purpose:** Protection, beauty, healing from heartbreak, divination
- ❋ **Planetary Ruler:** Sun
- ❋ **Elemental Ruler:** Fire

Witch hazel grows as a flowering deciduous shrub in many parts of Asia and North America. Despite the name, witch hazel isn't named for practitioners of magic; it's from the Middle English word *wiche*, which means "pliable." The bendable twigs of this plant are used as dowsing rods to find water or missing items.

Early physicians figured out witch hazel's astringent properties, so it's been used to treat skin problems from acne to eczema, and even hemorrhoids. Native American healers among the Osage and Potawatomi brewed the bark and leaves into a tonic to use as a sedative and painkiller, and to cure digestive disorders or postpartum bleeding.

MAGICAL USES: Use witch hazel to keep your house clean and safe with the Home Purification Wash for Floors & Doors (page 93). Burn a blend of the bark and leaves to repel evil influences. Carry witch hazel wood in a pocket to repel negative energy in crowds. Witch hazel is often associated with love, but you can use it in the Heartbreak Healer spell (page 109) to mend and move on from a relationship that ended badly.

Brew witch hazel into an infusion and add it to your bath or a face wash in beauty spells. If you're fortunate enough to find a witch hazel

plant, gather a Y-shaped branch and use it as a divination rod by holding the Y in your hands and following the stem for guidance; some people find this an excellent method to discover gemstones in the earth. Witch hazel is said to sway people to tell the truth, so keep a bit on hand if you want to guarantee an honest discussion.

Yarrow ....

- **Common Name:** Yarrow
- **Latin Name:** *Achillea millefolium*
- **Folk Name:** Arrow root, carpenter's weed, knight's milfoil, knyghten, lady's mantle, nosebleed, soldier's woundwort, stanch weed, tansy
- **Gender:** Feminine
- **Magical Purpose:** Healing, courage, love and lust, psychic powers
- **Planetary Ruler:** Venus
- **Elemental Ruler:** Water

Yarrow is found in many parts of the Northern Hemisphere, and it's been cultivated for medicinal purposes since medieval times because of its value in stanching the flow of blood from open wounds. In North America, many indigenous peoples used it as an analgesic to treat toothaches and headaches. A flowering perennial, yarrow produces tiny clusters of white flowers, and all parts of the plant can be used in medicine and magic.

Traditionally, yarrow is harvested on Midsummer's Day. **Yarrow is toxic to dogs and cats.**

MAGICAL USES: Use yarrow in spells for courage and confidence; carrying it on your person makes you fearless, no matter what challenges you might face. Use it in the Anxiety Jar (page 125). It's valuable in divination magic as well; in the Middle Ages, the flowers were brewed into a warm tea consumed to boost psychic abilities.

Long associated with love, yarrow can help you feel confident and appealing with the Herbal Beauty Glamour Spell (page 110). There's an old custom in which yarrow is rolled up in a piece of flannel and placed under the pillow at bedtime; by reciting a short poem (*Pretty herb of Venus' tree, your true name is yarrow, who of all my love must be, please tell me tomorrow.*) it's said that you'll be able to dream of your future lover. Once you figure out who your person is, hanging yarrow over your bed ensures a long and happy relationship. Hanging it over your bed during your honeymoon is said to guarantee at least seven years of happy marriage. Because of its association with medical uses, yarrow is popular in healing magic. Blend an infusion of one ounce of dried yarrow to one pint of boiling water and add it to your bath if you're suffering from joint pains.

~ PART THREE ~

Spells and Rituals

Now that you've taken the time to get to know some of the most commonly used magical herbs, you're probably wondering what in the world you can actually do with them! No worries—we've got you covered.

As you've learned, magical herbalism is an old practice, used for nearly every purpose under the sun. Whether you're doing a complex working to protect your home, a ritual bath to feel beautiful, or a simple grab-and-go spell to boost your finances, all of the spells in the next five chapters can be done using the 40 herbs we discussed in the previous section.

In addition to 15 different spells for each magical purpose— protection, love, healing, wealth, and divination—each chapter includes simple actions you can take any time to help bring herbal magic into your daily life.

**PROTECTIVE WREATH TO
GUARD YOUR DOOR**
page 92

CHAPTER

5

ᴘROTECTION

Have you ever been concerned about your physical or spiritual safety? They say one of the best defenses is a good offense, so why not use herbal magic proactively? By setting up protective magic around your home like the Herbal Braid (page 91), the Protective Wreath to Guard Your Door (page 92), and the Peaceful Protection Potted Plant (page 96), you'll be able to keep your house safe from trespassers and troublemakers. You'll learn how to protect yourself from magical shenanigans with the Purification Incense Blend (page 94) and the Home Purification Wash for Floors & Doors (page 93). If someone drops a smackdown on you, there's magic for that, too—one of my personal favorites is the empowering Magical Mayhem Jar Spell (page 98), which gives you back control of your life. Figure out what sort of protection you need in your life, open up your herbal pantry, and make some magic!

SIMPLE MAGIC ON THE GO

◆ Plant a combination of any three protective herbs in containers decorated with symbols of protection—the pentacle, an eye of Horus, a Hamsa hand, or a Mars sign are all good options—and keep them at your front door to filter out unpleasant visitors.

◆ Tuck a bay leaf in your shoe to protect you when traveling or add it into your suitcases to protect them from loss or theft.

◆ Hang garlands of herbs like lavender, pennyroyal, and eucalyptus around your house; they look decorative but also serve the valuable purpose of protection.

◆ Keep trespassers—or nosy neighbors—away by planting a boundary of hyssop, stinging nettle, and thistle.

◆ If you're worried about magical or psychic attack, use herbs like rosemary, dill, or peppermint in your meal preparations to help keep negativity away.

Protection Oil

Mixing up a magical oil is one of the simplest things you can do to protect yourself and your loved ones. Use this blend to anoint your pulse points or dab it on items you want to protect. You can even use it on magical tools—but be cautious with Tarot cards or notebooks that might stain or discolor when oils are applied.

* Pinch dried catnip
* Pinch dried comfrey
* Pinch dried hyssop
* Pinch dried vetivert
* ¼ cup carrier oil, like jojoba, grapeseed, or almond

1. Add the herbs to the carrier oil and swirl—don't stir—the oil in a clockwise direction; clockwise movement is associated with positive magic.
2. As the herbs blend together, say, *Herbs of protection, keep danger away. Watch over my home, night and day.*
3. Let the mixture steep a few hours, then strain and discard the herbs using a piece of cheesecloth.
4. Store your oil in dark-colored bottles to prevent spoilage. Use it to anoint yourself and your home.

Protection Pouch Sachet Spell

Make this simple sachet to tuck into hidden corners around your house, your dresser drawers or closets, or the cushions of your couch. No matter where you place it, it'll help keep your home and everyone in it safe from negative energy and magical or psychic attack from outside forces.

* White fabric cut into 2 [4-inch] squares
* Needle
* Thread
* Scissors
* Cotton or other stuffing material

- Pinch dried black cohosh
- Pinch dried dill
- Pinch dried feverfew
- Pinch dried valerian
- Pinch dried stinging nettle

1. Place the fabric squares together and stitch along three sides, leaving the fourth side open.
2. Use the open side to fill the pouch with cotton stuffing and your five herbs. Stitch the last side closed. As you do so, say, *Guardian herbs, protective herbs, watchtower herbs, protect this home and all who live within.*
3. Place the sachet in an inconspicuous spot to protect your family.

Protection Pocket Charm

Want some magic to take with you? Whip up this charm and carry it in your pocket, or give these as gifts to people you want to protect.

- ½ teaspoon dried peppermint
- ½ teaspoon dried rosemary
- Small piece of amethyst
- 3-inch square of red fabric
- Red cording or yarn

1. Place the dried herbs and the amethyst in the center of the red fabric, and gather the corners together to form a small sack.
2. Use the red cording to tie the top shut. Tie it tightly with nine knots. As you tie each one, say, *Protection and safety, peace of mind, herbs and stone, the magic I bind.*
3. Carry the charm in your pocket or wear it on a cord around your neck to keep yourself safe.

Herbal Braid

Display an herbal braid near the door guests use the most to keep negative and hostile people from entering your personal space. As the herbs dry, your space will be infused with their magical energy.

* Fresh chamomile stalks
* Fresh hyssop stalks
* Fresh lavender stalks
* White string or embroidery floss
* Decorative ribbon in your favorite color or design

1. Sort your herbs into three even groups. You can divide them by type, but it is not necessary to do so. Tie each group of stalks together at one end with the white string.
2. Braid the lengths of herbs together, forming a single long strand. As you're braiding, visualize the energy and power of the herbs enveloping your home like a shield, radiating out from the braid. Say, *Herbs times three guarding me, protecting my happy home. Preventing negativity, protecting my happy home.*
3. Once you've reached the end, use another piece of white string to secure it. Add a decorative ribbon, tied in a bow, at each end of the braid.
4. Hang your braids around your house for protective energy.

Basil Bath Bag

One of the most powerful protective herbs is basil. If you're concerned you're under a magical attack, curse, or hex, make yourself this bath bag. Use it in the tub to wash away negativity and ill magic.

* Muslin or cheesecloth drawstring bag
* Basil leaves—fresh is best, but dried will do

1. Fill the drawstring bag with basil.
2. Run a warm bath and hang the bag on the end of the faucet, so the water runs over and through the bag as it fills the tub.
3. Bathe as you normally would, and when you're finished, allow the water to run down the drain. Say, *Curse be gone, down the drain, may good come back to my life again.*
4. Bury the bag of basil somewhere far from your home.

Protective Wreath to Guard Your Door

You may prefer magic that doesn't scream, *Look at me, I'm doing spells!* at the family or next-door neighbors. If that's the case, home decor crafts are your best friend! Make this pretty and protective wreath to prevent danger and discontent from entering your house.

* Grapevine wreath, any size you like
* Fresh chamomile, lavender, and pennyroyal stalks, or any other protection herbs
* Ribbons, flowers, and other decorative items

1. Use the grapevine wreath as a base and weave your fresh herbs into the stems securely. Start at the top of the wreath and work around in a clockwise direction. As you do, say, *Circle round, circle round, my home is safe from the roof to the ground.*
2. Decorate your wreath with ribbons, bows, flowers, and other goodies, and hang it in your home near the front door.
3. Once the herbs have dried, remove them and save them for use in other protection workings.

Safe & Secure Smudge Sticks

Smudging, or the act of releasing smoke into the air, is a great way to purify a space. If you've moved into a new property—or want to revitalize the place you're already in—make these smudge sticks, light them, and send negativity away.

* Fresh chamomile, comfrey, lavender, rosemary, and rue stalks, 6 to 10 inches long
* Cotton thread or string, 5 feet long

1. Hold a bundle of your herbs so that the cut ends are aligned, and the leafy ends are all together.
2. Starting at the stems, wind the string tightly around the bundle, working your way to the bottom and back up. As you wrap them, **say,** *Protection and safety, these I call, to protect each room and every hall. Protection and safety, always known, keep ill will from this sacred home.*
3. Be sure to leave a bit of extra string so you can hang your smudge sticks up to dry. When they're completely dried out, light the end and use the smoke to clear a space of negativity.

Home Purification Wash for Floors & Doors

Have you recently had someone toxic move out of your home? The first step to eliminating their bad energy is to get rid of all their stuff, which is really gratifying. Then do a thorough cleansing using this home purification. For extra magical energy, create this on the night of the full moon.

* 1 tablespoon bay leaf, fresh or dried
* 1 tablespoon hyssop, fresh or dried
* 1 tablespoon rue, fresh or dried
* 1 tablespoon witch hazel, fresh or dried
* Drawstring cloth bag
* 1 gallon hot water

1. Place the herbs in the drawstring bag and add it to the hot water. Stir it in a clockwise direction to blend it.
2. Use the water to wash your hard floors and clean your windows. As you clean, say, *My home is sacred, my home is safe, my home is a sanctuary, and with this water, I cleanse it of ill intent and negative energy.*
3. When you've finished, take the water outside to dispose of it.

Purification Incense Blend

Burning incense is a great way to accentuate the magic of any ritual or spell. Blend this incense and light it as you're doing other protection or purification workings, or just leave it burning in your space as a stand-alone magical cleanse.

* Mortar and pestle
* Dried bergamot
* Dried catnip
* Dried eucalyptus
* Dried mistletoe
* Dried mullein
* Dried vetivert
* Fire-safe bowl
* Spoon
* Charcoal disc

1. Use the mortar and pestle to grind your herbs, one at a time, into a powder, releasing their fragrance and their magical energy. Combine the ground herbs in a bowl, blending them together by stirring clockwise.
2. Burn your incense in a fire-safe bowl on a charcoal disc. To purify a room or house, walk in a clockwise direction, carrying the bowl of burning incense, saying, *Sacred smoke, cleanse my space. Sacred smoke, purify this place.*
3. As the smoke rises, visualize it carrying negative energy with it, away from you and off into the universe.

Keep Your Car Covered Protection Charm

This simple car protection charm—which is especially useful if you have teen drivers—can be tucked into the glovebox, under the front seat, or even in the well beneath the spare tire to keep the vehicle's occupants safe from harm while they're out and about.

* 4-inch block of thick foam
* Utility knife
* Toy car representing the one you wish to protect
* 1 teaspoon dried cinquefoil
* 1 teaspoon dried mandrake
* Electrical tape

1. Cut a slit in the foam and insert the toy car. Stuff the herbs into the opening as well.
2. Wrap the entire foam block with electrical tape, covering the whole thing so that the toy car and herbs are securely tucked inside. As you wrap the tape, visualize yourself wrapping protective energy like a blanket around the vehicle that you or a loved one will be driving.
3. Place the tape-wrapped foam block in the car, in a spot where no one will notice it, to keep drivers and passengers safe.

Magical Protection Poppet

If you think you're under a magical or psychic attack, but you're unsure of the source, break out the big guns and build a decoy. This poppet will take the hits for you and keep you safe.

* Fabric
* Needle
* Thread
* Scissors
* Cotton or other stuffing material

* 1 teaspoon each of any three, dried:
  - basil
  - bay leaf
  - bergamot
  - catnip
  - comfrey
  - mullein
  - pennyroyal
  - peppermint
  - rosemary
  - rue
  - witch hazel

1. Cut two human shapes from the fabric to represent yourself. Stitch them together into a poppet, leaving a small opening.
2. Fill the poppet with cotton or other stuffing, and add your herbs. Sew the opening shut.
3. Say, *This poppet represents me and will take on any ills sent my way. This poppet will deflect any curse or hex sent to me. This poppet will absorb pain in my stead.*
4. Take your poppet somewhere far from your home and bury it. Any negative magic will be absorbed by the poppet and stay away from you.

Peaceful Protection Potted Plant

Do this simple protection spell to bring peace and harmony into your home. In warm weather, move your plant outside for sunshine and fresh air, but keep it indoors in cooler months.

* Potting soil
* Trowel
* Pretty flowerpot
* 3 hematite stones
* Rosemary seedling

1. Place a thin layer of soil in the bottom of the pot and add the **hematite, saying,** *Stones times three protecting me from any sort of negativity.*
2. Add more soil, and then gently place the seedling in the pot, making sure the roots are thoroughly covered. As you firmly pat the soil around the rosemary, say, *Fragrant stems and leaves of green, keep me safe from trouble unseen.*
3. Decorate the pot with symbols of peacefulness and tranquility. As your plant grows, so will the magic that keeps unpleasantness away.

Vervain Water

Vervain was a sacred plant in many ancient civilizations. Brew a batch of vervain water to cleanse magical tools, asperge around a sacred space, or purify your altar for spellwork.

* ½ cup fresh vervain leaves
* Pitcher or bowl
* 2 cups water
* Pot or tea kettle
* Funnel
* Wide-mouthed jar with lid
* Honey, stevia, or other sweetener, optional

1. Place the vervain leaves in a pitcher or bowl. Heat the water to boiling in the pot or tea kettle. Pour the boiling water over the vervain leaves.
2. Allow the leaves to steep for half an hour, and then strain them off. Use a funnel to pour the water into the jar.
3. Use your vervain water for cleansing and purification rituals, to consecrate tools and other magical items, or to designate a sacred area.
4. You can also add a bit of honey, stevia, or other sweetener to make this a delicious tea that will help you feel relaxed and safe.

Spell to Stop a Gossip

Know someone who just can't mind their own business? We've all encountered those troublesome people who thrive on rumors and lies. Do this spell to bind them from spreading any more malicious words.

* Scissors
* Thick pink fabric
* Paper
* Pen
* 1 teaspoon black cohosh
* 1 teaspoon stinging nettle
* Sturdy twine

1. Cut the fabric into the shape of a tongue. Write the gossip's name on the paper and place it on top of the fabric. Sprinkle the herbs on top of the paper.
2. Roll the fabric tongue up tightly, with the paper and herbs inside the roll.
3. Wrap the twine tightly around the tongue, binding it shut, and tie it with three sturdy knots. Say, *Out of sight, out of mind, your wicked words I now bind. Your talk will bring no harm to me, as I will, so it shall be.*
4. Take the tongue someplace far away and bury it. The person will no longer be able to harm you with their gossip and deceitful words.

Magical Mayhem Jar Spell

If everything's going wrong, and the *only* possible explanation is magic, it's time to strike back. To fight against magical or psychic attack, use this spell to empower yourself with some magical mayhem and return those negative energies right back to the source.

* Small glass jar with lid
* 1 tablespoon dried bay leaf
* 1 tablespoon dried thistle

* 1 tablespoon dried valerian
* Sharp objects such as rusted nails, razor blades, and broken glass
* White vinegar

1. Fill the jar with the herbs and sharp items—be careful handling them! As you do, imagine all the negative energy you've received bouncing back towards the person who sent it to you. If you don't know who they are, that's okay—simply focus on *The Sender*, rather than a specific name.
2. Pour the vinegar to the top of the jar, saying, *You have no power anymore; no further harm can you do. You will not hurt me anymore; all you send, I send back. I return to you all you use against me; I return to you all you give me, past, present, and future.*
3. Tightly secure the lid, take the jar somewhere far from your home, and bury it.

LOVE POPPETS
page 105

CHAPTER 6

LOVE

Spells designed to create and keep romance have been the staple of the local wise woman, the cunning man, and the village herbalist for ages. Read accounts of magical folklore, and you'll find frequent references to charms, talismans, potions, and amulets that people have used to draw love their way, with spells like the Cool Cat Love Sachet (page 103) or the Hey Baby Basil Magic working (page 112).

Remember, many magical traditions have guidelines against using love magic on specific people. Instead, focus on drawing love into your life with spells like the Lavender Love Incense (page 103) or the Pocket Love Charm (page 105). Regardless of your approach to love magic, remember that true love and beauty often begin with the way you feel about yourself—try the Self-Love Bath Bomb Bag (page 109) or the Candle Spell to Bring Love into Your Life (page 107).

SIMPLE MAGIC ON THE GO

- ◆ Obtain a piece of hair from the person you love. Wrap it in a piece of cloth and then carry the cloth in your shoe, and you will have a strong, powerful, and loving relationship.
- ◆ Bake a cake for the person you're attracted to, and as you pour the batter into the pan, use a spatula to draw a heart on the top. When the cake is done baking, frost the cake and give it to your lover to eat.
- ◆ Dab diluted patchouli oil on your pulse points to make yourself feel more attractive when you're out in social situations where you might meet a potential lover.
- ◆ Grow love-related herbs like lavender, rosemary, and peppermint in decorative pots around your home to attract love into your life.
- ◆ Chocolate is well known as an aphrodisiac; if there's someone you're into, offer a box of chocolate to show your love, and watch the sparks fly.

Cool Cat Love Sachet

Is there someone already in your life that you'd like to attract as a lover? Make this simple herbal sachet to boost the romantic potential, using catnip to bring love to your life.

* A 6-by-3-inch piece of red or pink fabric
* Scissors
* Needle
* Thread
* Cotton or other stuffing material
* 1 tablespoon dried catnip
* Piece of rose quartz
* Red or pink ribbon

1. Fold the fabric in half to make a square and stitch the two side edges closed, leaving the end opposite the fold open.
2. Stuff loosely with the cotton and add the catnip and rose quartz.
3. Use the ribbon to tie the bag shut. As you do, say, *Love come to me, love is drawn to me, love belongs to me.* Leave the sachet somewhere inconspicuous the person will eventually be near—for example, in their couch cushions, under their bed, or in a pocket of their clothing.

Lavender Love Incense

Lavender has been used for ages in magic to strengthen pure, romantic love and bring good luck in matters of the heart. Blend this incense and burn it during the waxing moon phase to draw romance into your life. While you're working on this spell, think about the sort of person you'd like to attract.

* ¼ cup dried lavender
* 1 tablespoon dried chamomile blossoms
* 1 tablespoon dried patchouli
* 1 tablespoon rosemary

* Fire-safe bowl
* Mortar and pestle, optional
* Charcoal disc

1. Combine your herbs in a bowl and mix them together. If you like, use a mortar and pestle to grind them and help release their magic. As you do, inhale the soft, romantic fragrances as they combine with each other and visualize loving energy surrounding you. Imagine the qualities you'd like to see in a potential lover—caring and sensitive? Adventurous and spontaneous? Do you want a partner who values physical touch, or are words more important?
2. Burn your incense on a charcoal disc, and as you light it, say, *By rising smoke, from earth to air, I call to me a lover fair. From the soil to the skies above, I call to me romantic love.*
3. Over the next few weeks, start paying attention to the people around you. Is there someone who fits your description of the ideal partner? Watch to see if they have any romantic interest.

Kiss Me Mouthwash Magic

Cinnamon is a fiery, passionate herb associated with high-energy love. If there's someone special in your life and you'd like to move things to the next level, blend this magical mouthwash mix to feel deliciously kissable.

* ½ cup hot water
* 1½ teaspoons ground cinnamon
* 1½ teaspoons honey
* ½ teaspoon baking soda
* 1 teaspoon lemon juice
* Wide-mouthed jar with lid

1. Place the water, cinnamon, honey, baking soda, and lemon juice in the jar. Place the lid on the jar and swirl in a clockwise motion to blend.
2. When you're about to encounter the person you're attracted to, swish about 2 tablespoons of your cinnamon mix around in your mouth to give yourself fresh breath and keep them coming back for more.

3. Store your mouthwash in the jar, and warm it up before each use to soften the honey.

Pocket Love Charm

High John root is found in Hoodoo and other folk magic traditions, associated with sexual prowess, fertility, and power—using High John means you'll have no shame in your game! Carry this love charm in your pocket to feel extra sexy and attract potential partners.

* Red candle
* High John the Conqueror root
* Red thread

1. Inscribe a heart shape on the red candle and light it.
2. As it burns, hold the High John root in your dominant hand and visualize it filling with self-assurance and vitality.
3. Wrap the root in the red thread, saying, *Power, strength, and energy, my confidence will draw a lover to me.*
4. Carry the root in your pocket and people will be drawn to your poise and charisma.

Love Poppets

If you already have a lover and want to spice things up, these poppets will give your romantic life a boost. Create a pair of them to represent both yourself and your adoring partner.

* Red or pink silk or cotton
* Scissors
* Fabric glue
* A photo of yourself and a photo of your lover
* Needle
* Thread
* Cotton or some other stuffing material

- 1 tablespoon dried patchouli
- 2 cinnamon sticks
- Red ribbon

1. Use the fabric to cut out four human shapes. On two of them, glue the photos of your faces on the heads of the poppet shapes.
2. Place the fabric in pairs, right sides together, and stitch around the edges, leaving an opening on one side to create two poppet figures.
3. Stuff the poppets with cotton filling and patchouli and then sew the openings shut. Place the poppets together, with the faces looking at each other, and put the cinnamon sticks between them.
4. Use the red ribbon to tie the poppets together securely, with the cinnamon sticks in the middle.
5. Place the poppets under your bed to add some romantic sizzle to your relationship.

Va-va-va-voom Valerian Oil

Although valerian has a strong odor that not everyone likes, it has been used in love magic for a long time. To attract romance, use this magical oil to anoint your pulse points. If possible, do this spell under the waxing moon phase, associated with attraction magic.

- 4 drops valerian essential oil
- 4 ounces carrier oil, such as jojoba, grapeseed, or almond
- Dark-colored glass jar or bottle with lid

1. Add the valerian oil and carrier oil to the bottle and cap the lid.
2. Swirl it gently in a clockwise direction. As you do so, say, *Love tomorrow and love today, I draw the ideal love my way. Love today and love tonight, the lover I welcome will be just right.*
3. Dab a bit of oil behind your ears, on your wrists, and at the backs of your knees to feel sexy and lovable to potential romantic partners.

Apple Blossom Countdown

If you find yourself torn between two potential suitors, use apple blossoms for love divination and do a quickie countdown to see who's likely to return your amorous intentions.

* Paper
* Pen
* Fresh apple blossoms

1. Draw a line down the center of the paper. On one side, write the name of your first potential lover. On the other half, write the name of the second.
2. Hold the apple blossoms in your non-dominant hand and close your eyes. Breathe in the scent of the apple blossoms and visualize the potential for love with each partner.
3. With your eyes still closed, use your dominant hand to scatter the apple blossoms in front of you, a few at a time, over the paper. As you do, say, *Apple blossoms, play my game, show me which is my true love's name. From my hand, on the paper to rest, reveal to me who loves me best.*
4. When there are no more apple blossoms in your hand, open your eyes and look at the paper. Whichever side has more blossoms on it is the person who is your true partner.

Candle Spell to Bring Love into Your Life

If you're tired of flying solo and want to let someone into your life, use this working to open yourself up and let the universe know you're ready to give and receive love from other people.

* Pink candle
* Carrier oil, such as jojoba, grapeseed, or almond
* Dried dill, ground into a powder

1. Inscribe the candle with the word *Love*, or images of hearts and other symbols that make you think of romance.
2. Dress the candle with the carrier oil and roll it in the dill so it's completely covered.
3. Light the candle and focus on the flame. Visualize yourself putting out loving energy, so the world knows you're ready to take the next step and welcome love. As you do, say, *I am worthy of love, I am deserving of love, I wish to love and be loved. I have value, I have an open and loving heart, and I am ready to share myself with a worthy partner.*
4. Continue visualizing love coming to you from someone who deserves all you have to offer.
5. Allow the candle to burn out on its own, and then bury it somewhere near your home to attract love into your life.

Patchouli Passion

Got your eye on someone special? This patchouli spell can send the message that you're an enthusiastic and sensual lover. Keep in mind it often brings passion when used alone, but not always long-term romance; incorporate apple blossoms into this spell to bring sweet romance as balance if you're looking for something that will last.

* 1 teaspoon patchouli
* 1 teaspoon apple blossoms
* Small bowl
* Spoon
* Small pink envelope
* Pen

1. Combine the patchouli and apple blossoms together in a small bowl, stirring in a clockwise direction.
2. Visualize the person you're interested in. As you do, say, *I am ready to love you, I am ready for you to love me, I am ready to have you in my life.*
3. Place the herbs in the envelope, seal it, and write your potential lover's name on it. Carry the envelope in your pocket when you know they'll be around; they'll see you in a whole new way.

Heartbreak Healer

Breakups are tough. No matter whose fault it was, or who ended the relationship, it's hard to bounce back. Do this working to heal a broken heart during the waning moon phase; this period is associated with banishing and getting rid of things.

* Photos, letters, or other paper items associated with the person who broke your heart
* Paper grocery sack
* Dried stinging nettle branches
* Dried witch hazel branches
* Bonfire

1. Gather up the photos and papers, and place them in the paper sack along with the stinging nettle and witch hazel.
2. Fold the bag closed at the top, and then fold it into the smallest packet you can make.
3. Light the bonfire. Once you have a good blaze going, place the bag and its contents right in the center of the flames. Say—or shout, if it makes you feel better—*I release you, I send you away! You have no more power over me! I have cut the ties, and I eliminate things and people who are hurtful. I release you, and I send you away!*
4. Once the bag has completely burned, allow the fire to burn out on its own. After the ashes cool, scoop them out and take them far away. Scatter them into the wind, so the memories of the person will no longer make your heart ache.

Self-Love Bath Bomb Bag

Let's face it, people are drawn to those who carry themselves with poise and self-assurance. This bath bomb bag will empower you to feel attractive, cool, and worthy of romance from those who deserve you.

* 1 tablespoon lavender
* 1 tablespoon mandrake

* 1 tablespoon vervain
* 1 tablespoon vetivert
* 10-inch square of thin muslin or cotton
* White ribbon
* Red candle

1. Place the herbs in the center of the square of cloth and gather up the corners. Use the white ribbon to tie it, forming a pouch.
2. Run a warm bath and hang the pouch over the faucet, allowing the water to run through it, filling the tub with the essence of the herbs.
3. Light the candle and climb into the tub. Allow yourself to soak in the warm, fragrant water. Use the herb pouch to wash your body; as you do, gaze into the candle's flame. Visualize yourself radiating an aura of self-confidence and power. See yourself as the sort of person who attracts attention from those who are worthy.
4. When the water cools, extinguish the candle and get out of the tub. After you've dried off, dispose of the herb pouch by burying or burning it.

Herbal Beauty Glamour Spell

They say beauty is only skin deep, but it's also in the eye of the beholder. That means it's often people's *perception* of you that's attractive. Try this glamour spell salve to create an aura of beauty, inside and out, and allow others to see you as the gorgeous creature you are.

* 2 ounces beeswax
* ½ cup coconut oil
* ½ cup olive oil
* Glass measuring cup
* Pan filled with water
* Spoon
* 10 to 12 drops lavender essential oil

* 10 to 12 drops yarrow essential oil
* Mirror
* Pretty tin or jar

1. Combine the beeswax, the coconut oil, and the olive oil in a glass measuring cup, and warm it in a pan full of water, creating a double boiler effect. Once the wax melts, stir everything until well blended, and remove it from the heat.
2. Add the lavender and yarrow oils, stirring them in slowly. As you do, look in the mirror and say, *I am lovely, I am desirable, I am magical. Beauty is more than skin deep. See me for the magnificence of my inner self.*
3. Before it cools, pour your salve into a pretty tin or jar. After it has firmed up, use it on your skin, and watch people start to notice you as they see you for the beautiful person you are within.

Fertility Amulet

If you want to improve your sex life, bring some extra passion into your bedroom activities, and possibly conceive, craft this fertility amulet to carry with you. Do this spell beginning three evenings before the night of the full moon, if possible. Remember, if you're having trouble conceiving, consult a medical professional for advice in addition to doing this spell.

* Dried mandrake root
* Bowl of warm water

1. Place the mandrake root in a prominent location in your bedroom, and let it sit undisturbed for three days.
2. At the end of the third day—ideally, during the full moon—place it in the warm water and let it remain there overnight. The root is now magically activated; place it under your bed or carry it as a pocket charm to encourage fertility and sexual passion.
3. To dispose of the water after the root is removed, don't just throw it away; sprinkle it at your doors and windows to bring passion and powerful energy into your home.

Rosemary Remembrance for Long-Lost Love

William Shakespeare wrote, "There's rosemary, that's for remembrance; pray, love, remember." Is there someone you once loved, and you just can't forget—the one who got away? This remembrance spell will help heal the heartache you've carried across the years, and release the person while you look back at the positive aspects of the relationship.

* 6 drops rosemary essential oil
* 3 drops peppermint essential oil
* 1 drop lavender essential oil
* White candle

1. Add the oils to the top of the candle, one at a time, in a clockwise direction around the wick.
2. Light the candle and gaze into its flame.
3. Visualize your fond memories of the person who has left your life. As you do, say, *I thank you for the time we had together, I thank you for the love we shared, I thank you for being such an important part of my life. We have parted, we move on, we remember. I wish you the best life has to offer and hope you have found happiness.*
4. Allow the candle to burn out on its own. Take the remaining wax and dispose of it somewhere away from your home; ideally, bury it in a place that you and your person made happy memories together.

Hey Baby Basil Magic

Basil is often associated with passionate love. In India, it's used in wedding ceremonies to ensure faithfulness and a prosperous marriage. Attract sizzling hot romance with basil. In addition to spicing things up, basil ensures your partner will be faithful.

* 1 cup fresh basil leaves
* 4 cups hot water

1. Steep the basil leaves in the hot water to create an infusion.
2. Allow it to sit for a few hours, until the water has completely cooled, and then strain the leaves out.
3. Spritz the cooled infusion on your bedsheets and pillows to ensure both desire and fidelity. As you do so, say, *Blessings and love, upon this bed, two partners sworn to one another. Basil fresh and leaves of green, bring about fidelity.*

HEALING INCENSE BLEND
page 117

CHAPTER

7

ᚺEALING

Healing herbs are a staple of magical practice; in fact, many aspects of magical herbalism evolved out of early holistic treatments for a variety of physical and mental ailments. While magic is certainly not a substitute for seeing a qualified healthcare professional, what it can do is make you feel better and promote overall wellness—use magic in tandem with medicine, not instead of it.

Try spells like the Healing Water Hand Wash (page 120) and the Happy Healthy Whole Poppet (page 123) to inspire good health, or the Stress-Relief Smudge Sticks (page 121) and the Anxiety Jar (page 125) spells if you're experiencing emotional distress. To battle colds, coughs, and fevers, make a batch of Healing Incense Blend (page 117) or a Feverfew Charm (page 118) to carry in your pocket.

SIMPLE MAGIC ON THE GO

♦ Hang healing herbs in bundles around your home to promote overall wellness—this is also a great way to dry freshly cut herbs for later use.

♦ Carry rue with you when visiting someone with a cold or cough; inhale the aroma to keep from catching what they've got.

♦ Keep a few aloe vera plants growing in pots in your home. If you've got a scrape, cut, or sunburn, snap off the end of a leaf, squeeze the juice out, and apply it to your skin for quick, soothing pain relief.

♦ Tuck soft, fresh mullein leaves into your shoes to relieve aching feet.

♦ Add lavender essential oil to a cotton ball and carry it in a locket. When you're run down and burned out, inhale the lavender to feel rejuvenated.

Soothing Sachet

Are you stressed, frazzled, and just plain fed up? Blend this herbal combination into a sachet to relieve anxiety and frustration. Use blue cloth, associated with healing of many kinds.

* Blue fabric cut into 2 [4-inch] squares
* Needle
* Thread
* Scissors
* Cotton or other stuffing material
* Pinch allspice
* Pinch eucalyptus
* Pinch peppermint

1. Place the fabric squares together and stitch along three sides, leaving the fourth side open.
2. Use the open side to fill the pouch with cotton stuffing and herbs. **As you do, say,** *Herbs of calm, herbs of relief, I blend you together to bring me peace. Herbs of quiet, herbs of serenity, I blend you together for tranquility.*
3. Stitch the fourth side closed. Place your sachet somewhere you go regularly to bring a sense of calm when you're overwhelmed.

Healing Incense Blend

Ill health doesn't just mean you've got a cough or a case of the sneezes. Sometimes, we're just feeling run down and achy, or blue and unmotivated. If you're under the weather, burn this incense for healing and overall wellness.

* Dried apple blossom
* Dried chamomile
* Dried mistletoe

* Dried peppermint
* Dried thyme
* Mortar and pestle
* Fire-safe bowl
* Spoon
* Charcoal disc

1. Place your herbs in a mortar and pestle one at a time and grind them to release their oils and magical vibrations.
2. Once your herbs are ground to powder, combine them in a bowl, gently stirring them together in a clockwise direction. As you do, say, *Heal my body, heal my soul, heal what's needed to make me whole.*
3. Place them on a charcoal disc in a fire-safe bowl and burn to relieve illness.

Feverfew Charm

When everyone around you is coughing and sneezing (and probably not washing their hands as often as they should), carry this feverfew charm to keep sickness at bay.

* 3 dried feverfew blossoms
* Small glass vial with stopper
* Chain or cord, 18 to 24 inches long

1. Place the blossoms in the vial, one at a time. As you insert them in the vial, say, *Illness will not come to my place, or touch my hands, or my face; with this charm, I will abide, sickness and ailments will stand aside.*
2. Seal the vial with the stopper and attach the chain or cord to the vial.
3. Wear it as a necklace if you're going to be spending time with people carrying seasonal diseases, or hang it over your desk to stay healthy at work.

Magical Mugwort Healing Dreams

Stress and anxiousness can manifest in different ways; for some, they lead to sleep problems. If you're so stressed out you can't get a good night's rest, do this spell at bedtime to bring about peaceful, healing images while you snooze.

* 1 teaspoon dried mugwort
* Your favorite mug or teacup
* 1 cup hot water
* 1 teaspoon honey, optional

1. Place the mugwort in the bottom of the cup and pour the water over it. Allow it to steep for 10-15 minutes.
2. Strain out the plant material and discard. If you like your tea sweeter, add some honey.
3. Drink your tea before you retire for the evening and you'll experience calm, soothing, restful dreams.

Safety note: Do not ingest mugwort if you're pregnant or nursing.

Spell to Soothe a Savage Cycle

When it's that time of the month, some people find themselves miserable, angry, and hurting. In addition to getting plenty of rest and focusing on self-care, do this spell to calm things down and promote inner healing.

* White candle
* 1 tablespoon black cohosh
* 1 tablespoon rue
* Small red drawstring bag
* Piece of carnelian
* Piece of moonstone
* Piece of garnet

1. Light the candle and gaze into the flame. Visualize your body healing and the pain and discomfort flowing out of you, going away with your monthly blood.
2. Place the black cohosh and rue into the pouch. As you do, say, *I am strong and healthy and will not let this cycle defeat me. I am strong and healthy and reclaim my body from the discomfort I feel.*
3. Add the crystals to the pouch, saying, *Red is blood, blood is life, life is power, and power is mine.*
4. Pull the drawstring closed and carry the bag in your pocket during your cycle to alleviate physical achiness and emotional imbalance.

Healing Water Hand Wash

Regular handwashing is one of the best ways to stay healthy. Use this healing wash to sanitize your hands, especially if you've come into contact with people who are ill.

* 1 tablespoon rubbing alcohol
* ¼ cup aloe vera gel
* Bowl
* Spoon
* 10 drops hyssop essential oil
* 2 drops peppermint essential oil
* Distilled water
* Cosmetic bottle

1. Mix the rubbing alcohol and aloe in a bowl, then add the essential oils.
2. Stir until thoroughly mixed, then slowly add the water until it reaches a consistency you like. As you blend it, say, *Fresh and clean, strong and well, I bathe my hands in good health.*
3. Store it in a cosmetic bottle and use your hand wash to keep your hands clean and germ-free.

Healing Oils Laundry Soap

When we're sick, our bodies tend to secrete unpleasant aromas that permeate our clothes and bedding. Wash your linens and garments in this magically fragrant laundry soap to help with healing and recovery.

* 1 gallon water, divided
* ½ cup each borax and washing soda (both can be found in your grocery store's laundry aisle)
* Wooden spoon
* ½ cup castile soap
* 10 drops eucalyptus essential oil
* 10 drops lavender essential oil
* Big storage container with lid

1. Bring ½ gallon of water to a boil in a large pan and then remove from heat. Add the borax and washing soda and stir in a clockwise direction.
2. In another pan, combine the remaining ½ gallon of water, at room temperature, with the castile soap and the essential oils.
3. Pour both mixtures into a large storage container with a lid and swirl them around to combine them. To wash your clothing or sheets, use ¼ cup of soap per medium load of laundry.

Stress-Relief Smudge Sticks

Anxiety and stress can take their toll on any of us—even those who think we've got a handle on everything. Burn this stress-relief smudge stick during healing rituals or to recharge your emotional well-being.

* Fresh lavender and peppermint stalks, 6 to 10 inches long
* Cotton thread or string, 5 feet long

1. Hold a bundle of your herbs so the cut ends are aligned and the leafy ends are all together.
2. Starting at the stems, wind the string tightly around the bundle, working your way to the bottom and back up. Leave some extra string so you can hang your smudge sticks up to dry.
3. When they're completely dried out, light the end and burn while walking around your house, and send anxiety, discord, and frustration away on the smoke.

Soothing Lavender Pillow

Feel like you're burning the candle at both ends? Make a dream pillow and bring about relaxing dreams, leaving you rested and rejuvenated in the morning.

* Blue fabric, cut into 2 [9-inch] squares
* Needle
* Thread
* Scissors
* Cotton or other stuffing material
* ½ cup dried lavender

1. Place the fabric with the right sides together and sew most of the way around the edges. Be sure to leave a gap on the fourth side.
2. Turn the material right side out, and stuff with cotton. Add the lavender, and stitch the opening closed. As you sew, say, *At night when I lay down to sleep, calming dreams come to me. Soothing lavender bring peaceful rest, calmness, and tranquility.*
3. Place the pillow in your bed and inhale the lavender's gentle aroma as you drift off to sleep.

Get Better Bath Spell

A nice warm bath is a great way to make yourself feel better, both physically and mentally. Not only does it help you feel clean, it also lowers your body's temperature, which is a real benefit if you're feverish. Use this bath blend for a long soak in the tub.

* 2 tablespoons dried bay leaf
* 2 tablespoons dried goldenseal
* 2 tablespoons dried rue
* Square of white cotton or muslin fabric
* Blue ribbon

1. Place the herbs in the center of the square of cloth. Gather up the corners, forming a pouch, and use the ribbon to tie it closed.
2. Run a warm bath and hang the pouch over the faucet, allowing the water to run through it and filling the tub with the essence of the herbs.
3. Climb into the tub and soak in the warm water. Use the herb pouch to wash your body; as you do, visualize yourself drawing healthy energy and well-being toward you, through your pores, and into every part of you.
4. When the water cools, get out of the tub. Pull the plug and let the water go down the drain, carrying illness away with it.

Happy Healthy Whole Poppet

Magical poppets, or dolls, have been used in healing magic for ages. If you're struggling physically or emotionally, make this poppet to bring wellness into your mind, body, and spirit.

* Blue fabric
* Scissors
* Needle
* Thread
* Cotton or other stuffing material

- 1 tablespoon dried aloe vera
- 1 tablespoon dried hyssop
- Felt-tip marker

1. Use the fabric to cut out two pieces in a human shape. Stitch them together into a poppet, leaving a small opening.
2. Fill the poppet with cotton or other stuffing and add the aloe and hyssop before sewing the opening shut. Draw a face on the poppet or write your name on it so that it clearly represents you, and say,
   I am healthy, I am happy, I am whole, healing my body and my soul.
   As I mend, I glow and shine, health and wellness now are mine.
3. Pamper your poppet—tuck it into a warm cozy bed, eat a bowl of chicken soup with it, talk to it while you sip a cup of hot chamomile tea—and soon you'll be on the mend.

Healing Wreath for the Sickroom

A popular healing modality in the past was to hang herbs in a sickroom. By using a circular shape—seen as powerful in many magical traditions—you have the bonus of sacred geometry in your workings. Make this wreath when you're under the weather.

- Grapevine wreath, any size
- Fresh healing herb stalks, such as eucalyptus and mugwort
- Ribbons, flowers, charms, and other decorative items

1. Use the grapevine wreath as a base and weave your fresh herbs into the stems securely, starting at the top and working in a clockwise direction around the circle.
2. Decorate your wreath with ribbons, flowers, and other goodies, and hang it over the bed in the sickroom to promote healing.
3. Once the herbs dry, take them outside, crush them between your fingers, and let the winds carry them away from you.

Anxiety Jar

There are many different causes for anxiety—if yours is a physical or mental health issue, be sure to consult a qualified practitioner. However, if your distress relates to your environment or current situation, use this jar spell to combat the angst. Channel your unease into the herbs and take the edge off your stress.

* Paper
* Pen
* Votive candle
* Small glass jar
* Dried stinging nettle
* Dried common thistle
* Dried yarrow

1. Jot down on the piece of paper the source of your stress, frustration, and anxiety. You can write, *My job has me stressed out,* or, *I just can't cope with any more family drama right now.*
2. Place the candle in the jar. Add the paper, and then the dried herbs on top of the candle.
3. Light the candle, and watch the paper burn, along with the nettle, thistle, and yarrow. As it does, say, *On this smoke I send stress away, frustration will be kept at bay. No more stress, no more strife, I banish anxiety from my life.*
4. Once the paper and herbs have burned away completely, scatter the ashes into the wind.

Healing Comfrey Candle Spell

Since there are few things as comforting as a candle spell, comfrey lends itself nicely to this working. Use a blue candle, the color associated with healing, to do this working when you're feeling tired, overworked, and down in the dumps.

* Blue candle
* Carrier oil such as almond, jojoba, or grapeseed
* Mortar and pestle
* Dried comfrey

1. On the candle, inscribe the words *calm, cool,* and *collected.*
2. Anoint the candle with the carrier oil. Using a mortar and pestle, grind the comfrey into a fine powder, and then roll the candle in it.
3. When the candle is thoroughly coated in the comfrey powder, light it. As the candle burns, visualize your body, mind, and spirit finding healing, peace, and tranquility. Allow the candle to burn down on its own.

Spell for Post-Trauma Healing

Many of us carry trauma within us, both physical and emotional. While trauma is complex—and won't be eliminated with just one magic spell—this working can help you focus as you heal. Do this spell during the waning moon phase and start banishing trauma, pain, and suffering from your life.

* 3 small strips of paper
* Pen
* 3 straight pins, thumbtacks, or small nails
* 3 black candles
* Black ribbon or cord, cut into three pieces
* 3 dried valerian stalks
* 3 dried stinging nettle stalks

1. On the three pieces of paper, write down words that describe the source of the trauma you're battling. It may be transgenerational, it may be emotional, it may be physical. Whatever it is, name it—*abuse, assault, pain, fear, addiction, etc.*—and be specific in your wording.
2. Use the straight pins to attach a piece of paper to each candle. Then, use the black ribbon to tie a stalk of valerian and a stalk of stinging nettle to each candle.
3. Light the candles one at a time. As they burn, shout out the words that are on the paper and banish them. Get angry if you need to. *Pain, I banish you from my life! Abuse, you have no control over me! Fear, I will not let you rule me!* Yell out your fury, your rage, all of the things you've bottled up, as many times as you like.
4. As the herbs burn with the paper, they'll help banish that trauma and guide you towards healing. Allow the candles to burn down on their own, and once they're out, dispose of them someplace far away so you'll never encounter them again.

PENNY POWER
page 135

CHAPTER 8

WEALTH

Since early humans first decided they wanted to acquire more stuff, there has been a desire for money magic. Whether we're talking about cash bounty or material possessions, there are endless ways to do prosperity spellwork. Whether you're looking to improve your financial situation by paying off debt, obtain your dream job, or build your own business, most practitioners believe wealth spells work best when performed from need as opposed to greed.

For overall wealth magic, try the Moneybags Money Bag (page 131) or the Cool Coin Purse (page 134); if you're a small business owner, look at the Cash Register Charm (page 135). To find gainful employment, use the Get the Jump on the Job Salve (page 139), and do the Check Your Wallet spell (page 131) to pay off a few extra bills each month.

Simple Magic on the Go

♦ Draw a dollar sign on a green candle and anoint it with a base oil. Roll it in powdered, dried goldenseal or patchouli and burn it during the waxing moon to boost your bank account.

♦ If you're gambling, carry a buckeye in your pocket for luck at the poker table or in games of chance.

♦ Sprinkle allspice in your shoes to increase your fortune and attract wealth.

♦ Plant chamomile and dill in a pot, draw dollar signs on it, and keep it at your desk, or wherever you normally reconcile your bank statements, to stretch your budget further.

♦ If you have career goals, write them on a chip or stick of sandalwood and burn it in a fire-safe bowl or cauldron. As it burns, your goals will be carried up to the heavens on the drifting smoke.

Moneybags Money Bag

Remember Mr. Moneybags from the old Monopoly board game? While this spell won't get you a swanky townhouse on Park Place, you can certainly make your own money bag to bring additional prosperity into your life.

* Paper sack
* Black magic marker
* Play money in various denominations
* Few drops bergamot essential oil
* Pinch allspice

1. Decorate the paper sack with dollar signs. Make them as big and fat as you like—the more the merrier!
2. Place the play money loosely in the sack.
3. Add the bergamot oil and the allspice. Then hold the top closed and shake the bag of money so that all of the bills are coated in the herbs. As you do, say, *Money comes, money grows, money earns, and money flows.*
4. Once you've finished shaking your money bag, walk around your home, placing the paper bills in various places where they'll remain undisturbed.
5. When you're done, fold up the empty bag and put it in a safe place. Your play money will soon draw real money into your home.

Check Your Wallet

If you have a blank check, write it to yourself and bring some extra scratch into your wallet. If you don't have a real check, create a facsimile with a rectangular piece of paper, a ruler, and a pen, or use your computer's printer to generate one.

* Blank check
* Pen

* 1 teaspoon dill
* Your wallet or coin purse

1. Ponder your list of bills or your regular budget and figure out how much you need to pay everything you owe this month. Write a check for that amount, made out to yourself.
2. Place the dill on the check and fold it up tightly. Tuck it in your wallet and leave it there to attract money to pay the bills.

Plant a Money Tree

The buckeye is associated with money and abundance. Although it doesn't grow in all climates, it thrives in many parts of North America. Plant your own and reap the financial benefits when the seeds start dropping. If you don't have a yard, start it in a container and move it to a permanent location later.

* Shovel
* Paper money, a single bill in whatever denomination you can afford to spare
* Buckeye seedling

1. Dig a hole deep enough to plant the seedling.
2. At the bottom of the hole, place the paper money. Say, *Like attracts like, money to me, growing in the roots of this tree.*
3. Place the seedling in the hole, fill it in with soil, and keep it watered and cared for. Within a few years, the tree will start growing buckeyes, and your fortune will increase.
4. Gather the nuts, dry them out, and string them to make wealth talismans to hang around your house.

Prosperity Pocket Charm

Prosperity and abundance can be found in unexpected places, and we often overlook financial boons that could be staring us right in the face. Keep this charm in your pocket to become more aware of wealth opportunities.

- 4-inch square of green flannel
- 1 teaspoon dried chamomile
- Piece of High John the Conqueror root
- Piece of twine or string

1. In the center of the green flannel square, place the chamomile and the High John root. Pull up the corners to make a pouch. As you do, say, *Money and fortune, come to me, with harm to none, so it shall be.*
2. Use the piece of twine to tie the pouch closed. Carry it in your pocket to draw bounty into your life in manners you normally wouldn't anticipate.

Mandrake Money Manifestation

Mandrake root can be hard to find, but once you do, you should take advantage of it to manifest wealth when you need it the most. Do this working during the waxing moon. If you can't find a whole root, use the dried leaves and bark for this working instead—simply place them in a bowl beneath the candle.

- Mandrake root
- Bowl of warm water
- Gold candle, scored horizontally in seven places

1. Place the mandrake root in a prominent location in your home, and let it sit undisturbed for three days. At the end of the third day, place it in the warm water and let it sit overnight. The root is now magically activated.
2. Place the mandrake root next to the candle so they're touching. Light the candle every night for seven days; as you do, say, *I manifest wealth, I manifest bounty, I manifest abundance, I manifest fortune, I manifest prosperity, I manifest means, I manifest money.*
3. Allow the candle to burn down to the score line each night. Before extinguishing it, drip a bit of the melted candle wax on the mandrake root.
4. After the seventh night, move the wax-covered mandrake root to a place of honor in your home to draw wealth and bounty.

Cool Coin Purse

Remember the old rhyme about finding a penny and picking it up, and all day long you'll have good luck? Use this coin purse spell to draw cash in, a few dollars or cents at a time.

* A shiny penny, nickel, dime, and quarter, all from the current year
* Small coin purse
* 1 teaspoon cinquefoil, fresh or dried

1. Place the coins in the purse and add the cinquefoil. As you do, say, *Penny, quarter, nickel, dime, extra money I will find. Penny, quarter, nickel, dime, extra cash will be mine.*
2. Carry the coin purse in your pocket or handbag, and whenever you see extra coins on the ground, pick them up and add them to your collection—when the coin purse is full, empty it and start again.

Penny Power

In many parts of the world, apples are associated with the harvest and, subsequently, bounty and prosperity. Do this spell during the waxing moon phase to take advantage of apple's properties of abundance in its many forms.

* Glass jar with lid
* Shiny new pennies
* Dried apple blossoms

1. Fill the jar with pennies and add as many apple blossoms as you can.
2. Cap the jar and say, *Pennies and money, grow beyond measure, money and pennies, increase my treasure.*
3. Bury the jar in your yard, and you'll draw more wealth your way. If you're fortunate enough to have an apple tree of your own, plant the jar beneath it.

Cash Register Charm

Owning a business is hard work, and sometimes it feels like there's little return on investment. Attract customers and encourage them to spend more money when you keep this charm near your cash register or workspace.

* Small box with lid
* 1 tablespoon dried dill
* Piece of High John the Conqueror root
* Small piece of citrine
* Small piece of tiger's eye
* Small piece of sunstone
* Small piece of gold quartz
* Gold yarn or thread

1. Fill the box with the dill, the High John root, and the crystals.
2. Close the box and bind it completely with the thread or yarn. As you do so, say, *Working hard to earn my due, fortune drawn, tried and true. Profit and gain is what I seek, in this cash register, full and deep.*
3. Place it in or near your cash register—if you don't have a cash register, discreetly tuck it someplace that your customers will have to walk past.

Bountiful Blessings Incense

Your idea of bounty and abundance may not necessarily be cash in hand—it could be material possessions, or the wealth that comes with knowing you're carving out a successful path for yourself. Burn this incense during money workings, or use it on its own to bring fortune into your life.

* Dried bergamot
* Ground cinnamon
* Dried goldenseal
* Ground vervain
* Mortar and pestle
* Fire-safe bowl
* Charcoal disc

1. Blend the herbs together, grinding them with a mortar and pestle. As you do, say, *Round and round these blessings go, as they turn, so they will grow.*
2. Light the incense on a charcoal disc, and as the smoke rises, say, *Up to the sky my intention goes, blessings return, and blessings grow.*

Patchouli Payoff Bath

Not everyone likes the earthy, rich scent of patchouli, but you'll begin to love it when it brings bounty into your life by letting you discard a negative financial mentality. By eliminating habits that give you an unfavorable impression of wealth or success, you'll open yourself up to a bright financial future.

* Patchouli essential oil

1. Run a warm bath and add a few drops of the patchouli oil.
2. Soak in the tub and think about the habits and behaviors that may be preventing you from achieving financial success. Do you think people who have achieved success are just lucky instead of hard-working? Do you view people with money as being evil? Visualize those negative concepts being broken and discarded.
3. Instead, focus your intention to attract prosperity, drawing abundance into your life. Think about the things you can achieve by making smart financial decisions and taking advantage of opportunities that might be out there. It can be hard if you're in a financial situation that's out of your control, so focus on the things you *can* control.
4. When you drain the tub, picture that unhealthy financial mindset going down the drain and being replaced by a positive economic outlook.

Beeswax Money Candle

In many parts of Asia and Europe, bees are a symbol of wealth and prosperity—they're also hard workers whose diligence pays off, so why not use their wax to make a pair of simple wealth-drawing candles?

* Mortar and pestle
* Dried apple blossoms
* Dried chamomile
* 1 (8-by-16-inch) sheet of natural beeswax
* 2 (4½-inch) candle wicks

1. Use your mortar and pestle to grind and powder the apple blossoms and chamomile. As you do, visualize abundance and fortune coming your way.
2. Cut the sheet of beeswax in half so you have two pieces measuring 4-by-16 inches. Sprinkle the herbs over the beeswax.
3. Place one of the wicks along the short side of a piece of beeswax and roll the wax into a cylinder. When you've finished, the herbs will be rolled up inside this taper-style candle with the wick in the center. Repeat the process with the other piece of beeswax and wick.
4. Burn these candles in a holder to attract prosperity to your home.

Wealth Wash for Your Home

There's something comforting about a clean home—and a sparkling home full of prosperity is even better! Make this wealth wash to clean your floors, doors, and windows to attract fortune your way.

* 2 gallons water
* Ground allspice
* Dried chamomile
* Dried patchouli
* Cheesecloth bag
* Lemon juice
* White vinegar

1. Bring the water to a boil in a large pot. Place the herbs in the cheesecloth bag and add to the water—use as much or as little of the herbs as you like, but use equal amounts of each. Allow the water to boil for 20 minutes and then cool.
2. Once it has cooled, remove the bag of herbs, squeezing it out thoroughly, and add the lemon juice and vinegar to the water—again, the amount you use is up to you, and is based on your smell preferences.

3. Stir thoroughly and use the water to clean your windows, doors, and hardwood or tile floors; if you have carpet, put it in a spray bottle and mist your floors, attracting money to your fresh, clean home.

Get the Jump on the Job Salve

Are you applying for your dream job? Remember, this is one of those cases where mundane work must be done as well: Update your résumé, make sure you have a professional outfit for interviews, and fill out applications in your field. If you have a chance to interview, use this simple salve to attract employment opportunities.

* 1 cup coconut oil
* Goldenseal
* Glass measuring cup
* Pot of water
* Cheesecloth
* Jars or tins with lids
* 2 ounces shaved beeswax

1. Add the oil and goldenseal to a glass measuring cup and place it in a large pot of water to create a double boiler.
2. Bring the water to a boil and then turn the burner down to a simmer. Let the oil and goldenseal infuse for an hour.
3. Use a piece of cheesecloth to strain the herbs from the oil as you pour it into a jar.
4. Warm your beeswax using the double boiler method. Add the infused oil and stir gently until the wax is melted and it's all blended together. Remove from the heat and pour into jars or tins.
5. Before an interview, give yourself a magical advantage by applying this salve to your skin.

Piggy Bank Money Magic

Remember how exciting it was to fill up your piggy bank and then finally empty it out to buy something you wanted? Be a kid again by drawing extra money into your world and stuffing that piggy bank to the brim.

* Brand-new piggy bank
* Red or gold paint markers
* Whole vervain leaves

1. Use the markers to decorate your piggy bank with symbols, runes, or words that represent money and abundance.
2. Crush the vervain between your fingertips and drop the leaves through the coin slot on the piggy bank; imagine those leaves are well-earned bills going into your bank account.
3. Visualize money coming to the bank as you state intentions like, *I will gain what I need,* **or,** *Money will fill this bank.* Place the bank where you'll see it every day—and every night, drop any spare change inside as both an offering to your piggy, and to form money-conscious habits.
4. Once your piggy bank is full, empty it and start over again—or get a new bank and just keep adding to the bounty!

Spread the Wealth Money Oil

By anointing your wallet, your purse, or even your skin with money oil, you can attract wealth. If you want enough to help yourself and others, use this oil to attract extra cash, and then pay it forward.

* Pinch allspice
* Carrier oil, such as almond, jojoba, or grapeseed
* Bowl
* Few drops bergamot essential oil

1. Combine the allspice with the carrier oil in a bowl, and then add a few drops of the bergamot essential oil.
2. As you swirl the mixture in a clockwise direction, say, *Drawing money, because fair is fair, what I don't use, I will share. Extra cash, when it lands, I'll place it in another's hands.*
3. Use the oil to draw dollar signs on your wallet or purse, your skin, or even your front door to attract money into your life. When it appears, do as you promised and spread the wealth to others who might need it.

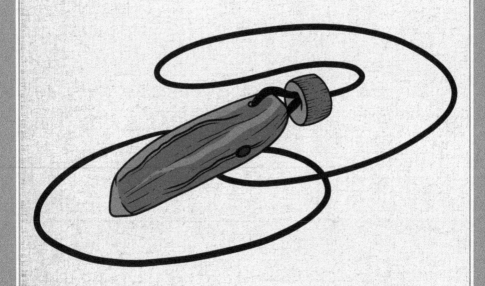

HERBAL PENDULUM MAGIC
page 153

DIVINATION

Divination is the practice of discovering knowledge via supernatural or esoteric means. It can take many forms: reading Tarot cards, tea leaves, pendulums, or scrying with a mirror or crystal ball. Divination magic can boost your skills and open you up to things that were previously unknown and unseen.

Use spells like the Mugwort Moon Magic (page 145) and Herbal Pendulum Magic (page 153) to answer specific questions, or the Awakening Oil (page 154) and Open Your Third Eye spell (page 151) to help broaden your divinatory horizons.

Simple Magic on the Go

◆ Keep a vase of fresh yarrow or mugwort wherever you do your divination work.

◆ Consecrate your divination tools with essential oil of vetivert to increase their psychic vibrations.

◆ Carry witch hazel bark or wood in your pocket to keep negative energy away.

◆ If you're doing divination work with ancestors or spirit guides, keep a bundle of rosemary handy to invite them in.

◆ Add cinnamon to any incense blend when you're doing divination work; it can boost your ability to connect to the spirit world.

Mugwort Moon Magic

Mugwort is a powerful divinatory herb used in sacred rituals of many religions around the world. Do this working outside during the full moon; if there's a problem you've been trying to solve, this working can show you all the possibilities, both seen and unseen.

* Large bowl filled with water
* Tall white pillar-style candle
* Fresh mugwort

1. Sit outside, placing the bowl on a flat surface so that when you gaze into it, you can see the moon's reflection in the water.
2. Place the candle beside the bowl, light it, and sprinkle the fresh mugwort across the top of the water.
3. Close your eyes and think about a pressing question or an issue that's bothering you. Speak your question out loud, three times: *How should I solve my problems at work?* **or,** *Do I need to end this unsatisfying relationship?*
4. Open your eyes and look into the bowl of water. Watch the moon's reflection moving in the surface and wait for messages or images that might answer your question.

Psychic Amulet

Many of us believe we have spirit guides. They may be ancestral, or perhaps ascended masters, or even archetypal guides. Although they often have messages for us, we don't always listen. Wear this amulet to attract visions, images, and messages from your spirit guides.

* Modeling clay
* 1 teaspoon ground cinnamon
* 1 teaspoon dried sage
* Necklace chain or leather cord, 18 to 24 inches long

1. Take a small piece of modeling clay and begin working it with your hands, rolling and kneading it until it's soft and pliable.
2. Add the cinnamon and sage into the clay, blending it with your fingers. As you do, visualize yourself opening your heart and spirit to communications from other realms. Shape the clay into a circle, ring, or other shape that makes you feel magical. Is there a symbol or rune you'd like to inscribe into the clay? If so, do it!
3. Allow the clay to dry, and then wear it on the chain or cord to enhance your awareness of messages from your spirit guides.

Basil Wisdom

Tasseomancy is the act of reading tea leaves to see visions and images. Using basil in a similar fashion, you can see what sort of messages are coming to you from the other side. Make a cup of basil tea and look for symbols and figures in the remnants at the bottom of the cup.

* 1 tablespoon dried basil
* Teacup
* Hot water
* Sugar, optional
* Plate

1. Place the basil in a teacup and pour the hot water over it.
2. Allow the basil to steep for a few minutes, and then sit quietly and drink your tea; as you drink it, focus on the specific problem to which you need resolution. Most people find basil tea a little bitter, so if you need to add sugar, go ahead, but don't add cream.
3. When you're done, leave a little liquid in the bottom of the cup, then swirl it around three times, and pour it out onto a plate.
4. You'll be left with blobs of wet basil—do they look like images? Do they form letters, numbers, or shapes? What symbols are in the basil leaves? Determine what those symbols mean to you personally, and how they apply to the question you asked, and you'll have guidance toward the answers you seek.

Herbal Scrying

Many people use smoke for scrying (it's as effective as fire or water) and tobacco has been welcomed as an offering and spiritual herb for a very long time. Blend it with some valerian, light a charcoal disc, and see what messages appear.

* Dried tobacco leaf
* Dried valerian
* Mortar and pestle
* Fire-safe bowl
* Charcoal disc

1. Grind the herbs together with your mortar and pestle, stirring clockwise.
2. Light a charcoal disc and sprinkle your herb mixture on top of it. As you do, say, *From earth to air, from below to above, I send smoke to the heavens, in light and love. I call upon my spirit guides, for answers that will no longer hide.*
3. As the smoke begins to rise, watch it move and look for images or symbols within it. Be sure to write down what you see so you can decipher and analyze it later.

Spiritual Bath Blend

Take a relaxing bath with this herbal blend to connect to your spirit guides. It will help you achieve a sense of deliberate psychic clarity.

* 8 cups water, consecrated, gathered during a storm, or blessed under the full moon
* Big pot
* Spoon
* 1 cup dried comfrey
* 1 cup dried mistletoe
* 1 cup sandalwood chips
* White candle

1. Bring the water to a boil on your stovetop.
2. Add the herbs one at a time, stirring in a clockwise direction. As you place each herb into the water, say, *I am awake, I am open, I am ready to see. I discard that which no longer serves me. I am awake, I am open, I am ready to see. I am prepared for the messages sent to me.*
3. Once you've added all three herbs, allow the water to simmer for a few minutes.
4. Draw a warm bath and pour the herbal infusion directly into the tub so you can soak in it. Light a white candle, and while you're in the tub, allow the flame to be your focus as you open your mind to receiving messages.

Divination Dream Sachet

Many people rely on dream messages for psychic awareness. Keep a journal or notepad near your bed, so that as soon as you awaken you can jot down your dreams. If there's an issue you need to resolve, make this dream sachet and sleep on the problem to get some answers.

* Yellow fabric cut into 2 [4-inch] squares
* Needle
* Thread
* Scissors
* Cotton or other stuffing material
* Pinch cinquefoil
* Pinch mullein
* Pinch rosemary

1. Place the fabric squares together and stitch along three sides, leaving the fourth side open.
2. Use the open side to fill the pouch with cotton stuffing and the herbs. As you do so, say, *As I lay down to sleep in bed, may visions and guidance fill my head. I'm seeking answers, both seen and unseen, and ready for wisdom in my dreams.*

3. Sew the fourth side closed and place the sachet under your pillow when you go to bed. As you fall asleep, focus on your questions. Your dreams will guide you in your quest for answers.

Thyme Teller Guidance Charm

Thyme is associated with guidance and wisdom, and black tourmaline helps you stay grounded. This charm will keep you focused, starting you on the path you need to walk—whatever it may be.

* 1 teaspoon dried thyme leaves
* Small drawstring pouch
* Piece of black tourmaline

1. Place the thyme in the pouch. As you do, crush it gently between your fingertips, so you can smell its rich fragrance, and say, *Thyme guide me, thyme lead me, thyme help me know.*
2. Add the black tourmaline, holding it in your palms and feeling its cool, stabilizing energy. Say, *Tourmaline ground me, tourmaline stabilize me, tourmaline help me grow.*
3. Place your charm someplace prominent so you'll see it regularly. Every time you walk past it, take a moment to hold it and absorb its wise, grounded energy.

Inspirational Intuition Incense Blend

Feeling like you've lost your mojo? Get your inspiration, creativity, and all-around spiritual spark back by burning this incense combination.

* Ground cinnamon
* Dried cinquefoil
* Dried mugwort
* Dried mullein
* Spoon
* Fire-safe bowl
* Charcoal disc

1. Blend all of your herbs together, stirring in a clockwise motion, and burn them in a fire-safe bowl on a charcoal disc.
2. As you watch the smoke rise, say, *Intuition, creativity, inspiration, wisdom, insight, perception. Come to me, come to me, come to me. Forward movement, rejuvenation, revitalization. Come to me, come to me, come to me.*
3. Allow the smell of the incense to permeate your mind, body, and soul, giving yourself a spark to get the creative juices and inspiration flowing. Take advantage of it immediately and go do something that makes your spirit soar.

Moonlight Divination Candle

The full moon is associated with wisdom, intuition, and hidden knowledge. Complete this simple candle spell under the full moon to get answers to your questions.

* Dried comfrey
* Dried sage
* Dried tobacco leaf
* Mortar and pestle
* White candle
* Carrier oil, such as jojoba, almond, or grapeseed
* White ceramic or porcelain bowl or plate

1. Grind the herbs to a fine powder in your mortar and pestle.
2. Anoint the candle with the carrier oil, and roll it in the powdered herbs to coat it.
3. Go outside under the full moon and light the candle. As it burns, watch the flame, focus on your question, and say, *Full moon guide me, full moon lead me, full moon show me what I need to know.*
4. Gently raise the candle, angling it slightly, and allow the melted wax from the candle to drip onto the ceramic bowl. Do this up to nine times, and when you've finished, look at the wax on the bowl to see what symbols and images appear. These will offer guidance and answers to the problem at hand.

Open Your Third Eye

The third eye is our key to knowledge of the divine. When it's open, you'll experience clear insight, a sense of open-mindedness, and a powerful connection to your inner guidance. Open yours with this simple meditative spell.

* Fresh mugwort sprigs
* Sandalwood chips
* Small drawstring bag

1. Blend the mugwort and sandalwood together and fill the bag. Lay down with your eyes closed and place the bag on the center of your forehead—the location of the third eye.
2. Allow your mind to clear. Visualize yourself becoming enlightened and aware, open to receiving messages from your spiritual self. Imagine glowing, pure white light pouring down from the universe, through the herbs, and into your third eye, filling it with energy and magic.
3. Let it envelop you thoroughly and say, *By the power of the universe's light, I claim intuition and wisdom. Open up the gift of sight. Open up my third eye. Open me to the messages I must receive.*
4. Do this to enhance your regular divination methods, like reading Tarot cards or runes, or do it as a standalone practice to become more psychically aware.

Self-Awareness Spell

Often, we spend so much time focusing on the needs of others that we forget who we are. By using positive affirmations, this spell will help you develop a stronger sense of self, even when you're tending the emotional and spiritual labor for everyone else in your life.

* Silver candle
* Paper
* Pen

* Mullein
* Stinging nettle

1. Light the candle, and on the paper, make a list of things you know to be true about yourself. Once you're done with your list, focus on the candle flame for a moment.
2. Go down your list and look at the things you wrote about yourself, paying extra attention to those that might be negative. Did you put down, *I get too emotional,* or, *I spend too much time at work,* or, *I worry about my family too much*? Cross those out and reframe them with a positive mindset: *I have a strong emotional connection to others. I am hard-working and dedicated. I value and cherish the way I care for those I love.*
3. Once you've revised your list so that it includes all positive affirmations, wrap the herbs in the paper, fold it into a secure packet, and then place it under the candle.
4. Take some time and meditate on all the things you wrote down, and remember that while they *describe* you, they don't necessarily *define* you.
5. Each day, review your list, and think about how wonderful and magical it is to be the person you are.

Clarity Smudge Sticks

It's easy to let our minds wander—but when you're trying to do divination, that's counterproductive. Light these smudge sticks to help bring you a specific sense of clarity and get to the bottom of whatever information you're receiving.

* Several fresh rosemary and sage stalks, 6 to 10 inches long
* Cotton thread or string, 5 feet long

1. Hold a bundle of your herbs so that the cut ends are aligned and the leafy ends are all together.

2. Starting at the stems, wind the string tightly around the bundle, working your way to the bottom and back up. Be sure to leave a bit of extra string so you can hang up your smudge sticks to dry.
3. When they're completely dried out, light the end and burn your smudge sticks, saying, *Clear sight, clear vision, clear awareness, these are the gifts that I give to myself.* Use during divination practices like Tarot, pendulum, or oracle card reading.

Herbal Pendulum Magic

Pendulums are easy to make and a lot of fun to use—anyone can put one together and make it work. Assemble this simple pendulum and use it for questions requiring a yes or no answer.

* Thumb-size piece of mistletoe wood
* Drill
* Cording, 12 to 14 inches long

1. Drill a hole through the short end of the mistletoe wood, wide enough to run the cording through it. String the wood on the cord and knot it securely.
2. To calibrate your pendulum, hold it steady and ask a question to which you know the answer will be *Yes.* See which way it swings—does it go side to side, back and forth, or in a circle? That's your *Yes* direction.
3. Now do the same thing with a question that you know must be answered as *No.* Once you understand which way your pendulum goes for *Yes* and *No*, you can ask divinatory questions to figure out the outcome.
4. You can also gather answers to questions by writing multiple options on a piece of paper and seeing which choice the pendulum swings toward—the answer lies in the direction of the pendulum's swing.

Awakening Oil

Craft this oil during the full moon to boost your psychic awareness. The more you awaken your abilities, the easier they'll be to tap into when you need guidance, and using them will become second nature for you.

* ¼ cup carrier oil, like jojoba, grapeseed, or almond
* Glass jar with lid
* Few drops basil essential oil
* Few drops thyme essential oil

1. Pour your carrier oil into a glass jar with a lid and add a few drops of the basil and thyme oils.
2. Swirl gently in a clockwise direction to mix thoroughly. Say, *I awaken, I listen, I see. Enlightenment come to me. Awareness, mindfulness, clarity. Illumination come to me.*
3. Anoint your temples and pulse points with your oil before doing divination work.

Sandalwood Clairvoyance Spell

Sandalwood raises psychic vibrations, so use this working to find that which you seek. If something's hidden away, unlocking your clairvoyant abilities will help you track it down.

* Loose sandalwood chips
* Fire-proof bowl
* 4-inch square of white cloth

1. Light the sandalwood chips in the bowl and allow the smoke to rise. Close your eyes and inhale its warm aroma. Visualize the thing you wish to locate—is it a person? A missing object? Something you'd like to draw into your life? Picture it clearly, and say, *From sea to sky, from forest to field, that which is missing will be revealed.*
2. Once the sandalwood has burned away, wait for the ashes to cool, then place them in the center of the cloth and knot the corners.
3. Bury the knotted cloth in your yard, saying, *From earth to air, from fire to ground, things overlooked will soon be found.*
4. Leave the knotted cloth in its burial spot until you find the thing you've been seeking; once you locate it, dig the cloth up, untie the knot, and clean it thoroughly for future use.

GLOSSARY

Altar: the sacred workspace in which magic and ritual are performed—a tabletop, cabinet, or even a spare table set up in a quiet place in your home or yard

Amulet: a natural object consecrated and then used for magical purposes

Anoint: the process by which candles or other items are rubbed with a thin coating of oil to prepare them for magical or spiritual work

Attunement: the process by which a practitioner becomes magically connected to the herbs used in a spell

Base Oil: the primary unscented and unflavored oil to which essential oils are added; used interchangeably with carrier oil

Bath: the practice by which herbs are used to wash or soak the body for magical purposes

Carrier Oil: used to dilute and extend the volume of essential oil used in a spell; used interchangeably with base oil

Consecrate: to bless an item for use in ritual or magic, cleansing it of past energy and influence

Correspondence: the manner in which an item represents another item or a concept by way of energetic properties or signatures

Elemental Ruler: the practice of associating plants with one of the four classical elements—earth, air, fire, or water

Enchantment: a method by which a plant is assigned a specific magical purpose in spellwork

Gender: the practice of associating plants with characteristics that are considered traditionally masculine or feminine

Incantation: a chant or mantra said during the preparation or performance of a spell

Incense: herbs, resins, or spices burned for their magical properties or for aromatherapy

Infusion: a liquid brewed by steeping the leaves, roots, and flowers of a plant in water

Magical Intention: the purpose or goal for which a spell is performed

Mortar and Pestle: a set of implements used to grind and crush herbs—the mortar is a bowl or flat surface, and the pestle is held in the hand to do the work

Ointment: a smooth, creamy preparation applied to the skin for magical purposes

Pendulum: a weighted item on a chain or string, used for simple divination spells and rituals

Pillow: a closed fabric vessel stuffed with herbs and other magical items

Planetary Ruler: the association of a plant to a specific planet, based on qualities and characteristics

Poppet: a magical doll used in spellwork to represent the person for whom the spell is intended

Potion: a liquid made of herbs with healing, poisonous, or other magical properties

Sachet: a cloth bag stuffed with herbs and other magical items

Scrying: divination performed by looking into a reflective surface

Signature: the magical energy vibration of an herb, crystal, or other item

Steep: to soak herbs or flowers in water to extract the flavor and soften the plant material

Sympathetic Magic: magic in which actions are performed upon one thing that symbolically represents something else

Talisman: an object that is assigned magical powers

Visualization: focusing the mind to see the end goal that should be achieved

Waning Moon: the phase of the moon leading from full back to dark, or new

Waxing Moon: the phase of the moon leading from new, or dark, to full

RESOURCES

Herbs

The Monterey Bay Spice Company (herbco.com) has hundreds of herbs and spices, many of them hard to find, at reasonable prices, sourced directly from farmers and growers. They offer wholesale discounts for larger quantities.

Mountain Rose Herbs (mountainroseherbs.com) offers some of the best herbs on the market for magical practitioners, aromatherapists, and chefs alike, available in bulk and ethically sourced.

Books

Paul Beyerl's *A Compendium of Herbal Magick* (Phoenix Publishing, 1998) is packed with more than 300 herbs and their magical and spiritual uses, with documented historical support.

Scott Cunningham's *Magical Herbalism: The Secret Craft of the Wise* (Llewellyn Publications, 1982) is one of the most hands-on and comprehensive books on getting started with magical herbs and their uses and is an invaluable resource for beginners and veterans alike.

Organizations

The American Herbalists Guild (americanherbalistsguild.com) is an association of herbal practitioners that offers webinars, classes, and other educational resources for anyone interested in learning more about modern herbalism, both medical and magical.

The Herbal Academy (theherbalacademy.com) has numerous programs available to help you learn about herbalism as both an art and a science and values sustainability and stewardship of the world's plant resources.

CommonWealth Center for Holistic Herbalism (commonwealthherbs.com), based in Boston, has a valuable collection of resources for learning about the scientific aspects of herbalism.

References

Blackthorn, Amy. *Blackthorn's Botanical Magic: The Green Witch's Guide to Essential Oils for Spellcraft, Ritual and Healing*. Newburyport, MA: Red Wheel/Weiser, 2018.

Cameron, Malcolm Laurence. *Anglo-Saxon Medicine*. Cambridge, UK: Cambridge University Press, 1993.

Covey, Hebert C. *African American Slave Medicine*. Lanham, MD: Lexington Books, 2007.

Culpeper, Nicholas. *Complete Herbal and English Physician*. Manchester: Gleave and Son, 1826.

Cunningham, Scott. *Cunningham's Encyclopedia of Magical Herbs*. Woodbury, MN: Llewellyn Publications, 1985.

Cunningham, Scott. *The Truth About Herb Magic*. Woodbury, MN: Llewellyn Publications, 1993.

Dugan, Ellen. *Garden Witchery: Magick from the Ground Up*. Woodbury, MN: Llewellyn Publications, 2013.

Faraone, Christopher. *Magika Hiera: Ancient Greek Magic and Religion*. Cary, NC: Oxford University Press, 1991.

Grieve, Maud M. *A Modern Herbal*. Stone Basin Books, 2015.

Hong, Seung Wook et al. "Aloe Vera is Effective and Safe in Short-term Treatment of Irritable Bowel Syndrome: A Systematic Review and Meta-analysis." *Journal of Neurogastroenterology and Motility* 24, no. 4 (2018): 528-535. doi:10.5056/jnm18077.

Murphy, Trevor. *Pliny the Elder's Natural History: The Empire in the Encyclopedia*. Cary, NC: Oxford University Press, 2004.

Murphy-Hiscock, Arin. *The Green Witch*. Riverside, NJ: Simon & Schuster, 2017.

Oesterley, W. O. E. *The Wisdom of Solomon*. Whitefish, MT: Kessinger, 2004.

Riddle, John M. *Dioscorides on Pharmacy and Medicine*. Austin, TX: University of Texas Press, 1986.

Roth, Harold. *The Witching Herbs*. Newburyport, MA: Red Wheel/ Weiser, 2017.

Sumner, Judith. *American Household Botany*. Portland: Timber Press, 2004.

Toll, Maia. *The Illustrated Herbiary*. North Adams, MA: Storey Publishing, 2018.

Tompkins, Peter, and Christopher Bird, *The Secret Life of Plants*. New York: Harper & Row, 1973.

INDEX

ACKNOWLEDGMENTS

This book wouldn't have come close to being possible if it weren't for all of the wonderful people in my life who have shared their magical knowledge with me over the decades. There are too many of you to name here, but if you think I'm talking about you, I probably am. Also, Beth Carman, Byron Ballard, Amy Blackthorn, Angie Kunschmann, and Lisa Wagoner—thank you for your love and witchy ideas, and for keeping me from setting my hair on fire when I found myself at a loss for words. Finally, gratitude to my Bitch Posse—Cathy, Shari, Wendy, and Mandy—for hilarious memes, GIF wars, breakfasts, and overall emotional support, because every adult woman needs a Bitch Posse. I love you all more than even chocolate, and I'm so thankful you're part of my tribe.

ABOUT THE AUTHOR

PATTI WIGINGTON first embraced Pagan spirituality in 1987 and works as an educator and workshop facilitator in her local Pagan community. She has been the editor of the Paganism & Wicca pages at LearnReligions.com (formerly About.com) since 2007, and her work has appeared in a number of other Pagan magazines, anthologies, and websites. She is licensed Pagan clergy and is the founder of Clan of the Stone Circle, a Celtic Pagan tradition.

Patti has a B.A. in history from Ohio University and is the author of *The Good Witch's Daily Spell Book*, *Wicca Practical Magic*, and *The Daily Spell Journal*. She shares her home with a pair of college students, several dozen Tarot decks, and a very large dog. You can find Patti online at pattiwigington.com or Facebook.com/aboutpaganism.

CPSIA information can be obtained
at www.ICGtesting.com
Printed in the USA
BVHW091402051121
620467BV00001B/1